INSIGHT'S
BIBLE APPLICATION GUIDE
Genesis – Deuteronomy

A LIFE LESSON FROM EVERY CHAPTER

From the Bible-Teaching Ministry of
CHARLES R. SWINDOLL

Insight's Bible Application Guide: Genesis–Deuteronomy
A Life Lesson from Every Chapter
From the Bible-Teaching Ministry of Charles R. Swindoll

Charles R. Swindoll has devoted his life to the clear, practical teaching and application of God's Word and His grace. A pastor at heart, Chuck has served as senior pastor to congregations in Texas, Massachusetts, and California. Since 1998, he has served as the founder and senior pastor-teacher of Stonebriar Community Church in Frisco, Texas, but Chuck's listening audience extends far beyond a local church body. As a leading program in Christian broadcasting since 1979, *Insight for Living* airs in major Christian radio markets around the world, reaching people groups in languages they can understand. Chuck's extensive writing ministry has also served the body of Christ worldwide and his leadership as president and now chancellor of Dallas Theological Seminary has helped prepare and equip a new generation for ministry. Chuck and Cynthia, his partner in life and ministry, have four grown children and ten grandchildren.

Published By:
IFL Publishing House
A Division of Insight for Living Ministries
Post Office Box 251007
Plano, Texas 75025-1007

Editor in Chief: Cynthia Swindoll, President, Insight for Living
Executive Vice President: Wayne Stiles, Th.M., D.Min., Dallas Theological Seminary
Writers: John Adair, Th.M., Ph.D., Dallas Theological Seminary
Terry Boyle, Th.M., Ph.D., Dallas Theological Seminary
Derrick G. Jeter, Th.M., Dallas Theological Seminary
Malia E. Rodriguez, Th.M., Dallas Theological Seminary
Wayne Stiles, Th.M., D.Min., Dallas Theological Seminary
Content Editor: Amy L. Snedaker, B.A., English, Rhodes College
Copy Editors: Jim Craft, M.A., English, Mississippi College
Kathryn Merritt, M.A., English, Hardin-Simmons University
Project Coordinator, Creative Ministries: Noelle Caple, M.A., Christian Education, Dallas Theological Seminary
Project Coordinator, Publishing: Melissa Cleghorn, B.A., University of North Texas
Proofreader: Paula McCoy, B.A., English, Texas A&M University-Commerce
Art Director: Mike Beitler, B.F.A., Graphic Design, Abilene Christian University
Designer: Margaret Gulliford, B.A., Graphic Design, Taylor University
Production Artist: Nancy Gustine, B.F.A., Advertising Art, University of North Texas

ISBN: 978-1-57972-966-0
Printed in the United States of America

Table of Contents

A Letter from Chuck

Application is the name of the game . . . at least it is in my calling. Without the application of biblical truth, a sermon can't rightfully be called a sermon; it's a lecture. This is why I tell preachers-in-training and young pastors that, as they study a passage of Scripture, they must *write down* the timeless truth or universal principle from the passage that will be applied in their sermon. If they can't boil down the essence of their sermon in a *practical* sentence or two, then these young preachers haven't created a sermon. They may have a collection of interesting and accurate thoughts, but they don't have a sermon—not without the application of a timeless truth.

But application isn't just the name of the game for the preacher. It's the ultimate goal for everyone who studies the Bible.

Defining application is simple. It's the answer to the question: *What difference does this timeless truth make in my life?* Putting application into practice, however, is a bit more challenging—for preacher and listener alike.

This is especially true when we come to the Old Testament. It's easy to understand and apply the story of Joseph fending off sexual temptation in the book of Genesis or even the Ten Commandments found in Exodus and Deuteronomy. We've all felt the hot breath of lust; we all know that murder is not good but honoring our parents is. But what do we do with the laws regulating Hebrew sacrifice in the book of Leviticus or the genealogies found in Numbers? What difference do those ancient passages make in our modern-day lives?

The answers to those questions are found in this book, *Insight's Bible Application Guide: Genesis – Deuteronomy*. This first volume in its series takes you through every chapter in the first five books in the Bible, including those obscure and difficult sections in Leviticus and Numbers. Future volumes will guide you through the timeless truths and applications of the Historical, Wisdom, and Prophetic Books of the Old Testament, as well as the Gospels and the Epistles in the New Testament. In total, the *Insight's Bible Application Guide* series will cover every chapter in all sixty-six books of the Bible.

In every age, application has been the name of the game. James admonished his readers: "Prove yourselves doers of the word, and not merely hearers" (James 1:22). This book is intended to help you do just that — to apply God's Word to your daily life. So let's not just hear and read the Word; let's apply it . . . let's do the Word, and let's do it today.

Charles R. Swindoll

About the Writers

"Genesis" by Derrick G. Jeter

A graduate of Dallas Theological Seminary, Derrick's passion is to exhort believers to understand and apply the Scriptures and to engage unbelievers with the truth of Christ's death and resurrection. Derrick presently serves as a writer for Insight for Living Ministries. He lives in McKinney, Texas, with his wife, Christy, and their five children.

"Exodus" by John Adair

John received his bachelor's degree from Criswell College and his master of theology degree from Dallas Theological Seminary, where he also completed his Ph.D. in historical theology. He serves as a writer in the Creative Ministries Department of Insight for Living Ministries. John, his wife, Laura, and their three children reside in Frisco, Texas.

"Leviticus" by Wayne Stiles

After serving in the pastorate for fourteen years, Wayne joined the staff at Insight for Living Ministries and currently serves as executive vice president and chief content officer. He received his master of theology and doctor of ministry degrees from Dallas Theological Seminary. Wayne and his wife, Cathy, live in Aubrey, Texas, and have two daughters.

"Numbers" by Terry Boyle

Terry serves as pastor for Insight for Living United Kingdom. His ministry involves hosting the daily *Insight for Living* radio broadcast throughout the UK and Europe, helping with theological or spiritual issues that come in from listeners, and providing a personal and local approach to Chuck Swindoll's international Bible-teaching ministry.

Terry was born in Windsor, England. He holds a master of theology degree in pastoral ministry and a Ph.D. in biblical studies from Dallas Theological Seminary. He served as senior pastor of Skillman Bible Church in Dallas, Texas, until he and his family moved back to the United Kingdom in 2007.

"Deuteronomy" by Malia E. Rodriguez

Malia received her master of theology degree from Dallas Theological Seminary and currently serves as a writer in the Creative Ministries Department of Insight for Living Ministries. She lives in McKinney, Texas, with her husband, Matt, who is also a master of theology graduate from Dallas Theological Seminary.

What Is the Value of the Mosaic Law Today?

Have you ever read through the first five books of the Old Testament, the books of the Law, and wondered, *What does this have to do with me?* Much of the Law seems foreign to our own experience, while other parts seem no longer to apply. Would Christians today ever consider selling our daughters into slavery (Exodus 21:7)? Do we expect to sacrifice a goat as a peace offering to God (Leviticus 3:12)? Or should we all go out and add tassels to our garments (Numbers 15:38)? How should today's believer handle laws such as these? Arriving at an answer will require us to expand our search, from the narrow valley of the Mosaic Law to the broad expanse of Scripture as a whole.

We begin our expedition in Paradise—the garden of Eden, to be exact. Here, in this place of perfection and goodness, dwelt Adam and Eve, the first humans. And before long, these two broke the single prohibition God had given them—they ate from the Tree of the Knowledge of Good and Evil. They fell into sin, choosing a path of rebellion against their Creator. Since that first couple, every human being has been tainted with sin.

Once we understand humanity's condition, we can better make the long journey to understanding Paul's foundational statement that the Law "was added because of transgressions" (Galatians 3:19). The Law was designed to make clear to people how they had sinned against God, as well as explain to them the means to get their relationships with God back in order. The Law, therefore, shows God's people—then and now—that we are sinners in need of God's grace. So when Jesus called Himself the fulfillment of the Law, He did so because He showed us what it meant to live in right relationship with God (Matthew 5:17). In addition, as sinners we can come to God for atonement and redemption through Christ (Hebrews 9:11–14).

When, on the cross, Jesus became the ultimate sacrifice for sin, humanity no longer required the sacrifices that God laid out in the Law. However, this does not make the Law useless to us. In fact, Paul called the Law "good" (1 Timothy 1:8). How, then, do we apply it?

Rather than making tassels for our garments or killing goats, we can learn from the Law by examining the principles that undergird it to discover more about the relationship between God and His people. The principles we glean from the Law can help us in our own lives with God. For example, when we see regulations regarding daughters sold into slavery in Exodus 21, we can perceive behind the specific laws God's concern for the welfare of women and for those without options in society — His desire that they be cared and provided for. When we read of goats being sacrificed for a peace offering, we are led to depend even more on Jesus, who brought peace between God and humanity through the sacrificial offering of His own life. And when we read a command about wearing tassels on garments, we understand that God expects His people to be set apart, sanctified for His work in the world.

On our journey to understand and apply the Law, we can see that it had a good function in the Old Testament era, offering people the means to recognize personal sin and make right their relationships with God. The Mosaic Law continues to have a good function today, making clear through its principles what God values and what we should value as we seek to follow Him.

INSIGHT'S
BIBLE APPLICATION GUIDE
Genesis – Deuteronomy

Genesis

Genesis 1

In the beginning God created the heavens and the earth.

—Genesis 1:1

The Bible starts where the Bible should start—with God, His Word, and His creative activities in the world. The first chapter of Genesis is a summary of the central message of the Bible: God is the sovereign Creator/Sustainer, Redeemer, and Lawgiver, and all He does is good (Genesis 1:31). We who live after sin's corruption of creation, however, don't always see God's creation as good. Rather, the natural world can be dark and dangerous. Yet creation wasn't always corrupt; it was once good and beautiful—and it will be again in the future. Just as God redeemed that which was dark, "formless and void" with light and life at the beginning of creation (1:2), so He will redeem His creation at the end of history when He makes all things new (Revelation 21:5). For now, we continue to trust in the Creator's goodness, waiting with faith and hope until creation is made whole again.

Genesis 2

For this reason a man shall leave his father and his mother, and be joined to his wife; and they shall become one flesh. —Genesis 2:24

Human beings stand unique in God's creation as the only creatures who carry the privilege and responsibility of the *Imago Dei*—of being created in God's image (Genesis 1:27). The first man, Adam, was created from the dust of the earth, made an eternal being, and given the tasks of tending God's garden and naming the animals. But Adam was alone. He had no one with whom to share in his uniqueness as God's image bearer. And this was not good (2:18). So God created Eve. In doing so, God established the bond of intimate relationship between one man and one woman within marriage (2:23–24). In our day, as the foundation of marriage becomes ever more porous due to the seepage of progressive and non-biblical ideas, we can remember and stand up for God's original concept of marital intimacy: two human beings of the opposite sex, for life.

Genesis 3

"Who told you that you were naked? Have you eaten from the tree of which I commanded you not to eat?" —*Genesis 3:11*

The contrast between Genesis 2 and Genesis 3 couldn't be more stark and shocking. The former is the account of Paradise gained; the latter is the account of Paradise lost. Where Adam and Eve had life, they now had death; where closeness, now distance; where abundance, now meagerness; where joyful labor, now sweat-ridden toil; where pleasure, now pain; where fellowship with God, now alienation from God. In Eve's misrepresentation of God's Word and Adam's passivity in leading his wife spiritually, the first couple doubted God's goodness and disobeyed His command. When confronted with their sin, Adam blamed Eve, Eve blamed the serpent, and both, by implication, blamed God (Genesis 3:12–13). But God's question to Adam (3:11) was an opportunity for Adam to accept responsibility and confess his sin. God gives us the same chance. And if we confess, we have confidence that He will forgive us, restoring our fellowship with Him (1 John 1:9).

Genesis 4

"If you do well, will not your countenance be lifted up? And if you do not do well, sin is crouching at the door; and its desire is for you, but you must master it." —*Genesis 4:7*

Sin couldn't be contained within the hearts and lives of just Adam and Eve. Like a wild animal refusing bondage, sin prowled through the hearts of their children and their children's children, until it devoured the whole human race. Angry because God rejected his offering, Cain rejected God's call for righteousness, took vengeance on his brother by murdering him, and received a just punishment (Genesis 4:6–14). But Cain's sin didn't stop with him. Four generations later, Cain's grandson, Lamech, multiplied his grandfather's sin (4:23). The story of Cain and Abel and the growth of civilization establishes three timeless truths: sin is a plague that spreads from families to societies and grows worse; we can choose the way of belief or the way of unbelief; and civilization is preserved through pleasing the Lord, obeying His commands, and calling upon His name. Our civilization today still needs faithful followers of God.

Genesis 5

Enoch walked with God; and he was not, for God took him.
—*Genesis 5:24*

Though Adam and Eve were fruitful, death was equally fruitful (Genesis 5:31). Sin entered the bloodstream of humanity and spread the curse of death to subsequent generations. An exception to the birth-life-death cycle was Enoch, who "walked with God" (5:22, 24). In the midst of a perverted generation, Enoch obeyed the commands of God, maintained intimate fellowship with God, and warned others of coming judgment from God (Jude 1:14–15). For this, God chose to overrule the curse of death and remove Enoch to heaven (Genesis 5:24). Death is a universal curse for sin, but death is not the final answer. As humans, we can do nothing about sin and death. But like Enoch, we can walk with God in faithfulness. And we can take every opportunity to tell others about Christ, the one who did do something about sin and death—He conquered them completely (1 Corinthians 15:56–57).

Genesis 6

Noah was a righteous man, blameless in his time; Noah walked with God. —*Genesis 6:9*

As generations grew, fulfilling God's first command (Genesis 1:28), so did evil. Ten generations transpired from Adam to Noah, and the Lord observed the depths of wickedness in the human heart. Such evil corrupted all of God's creation. For this the Lord grieved and pronounced judgment on the earth. Only Noah found favor in God's eyes (6:9). God chose, therefore, through divine grace, to preserve a remnant of His creation through Noah and his family. Our generation is just as wicked as Noah's generation. And like Noah's, no one in our generation will escape judgment—all will die and will have to present themselves to the living Lord who will make eternal judgments between eternal life and eternal death. But until that day comes, may we, like Noah, proclaim righteousness in word and deed to the unsaved, our families, our friends, and our neighbors (2 Peter 2:5).

Genesis 7

*Then the L*ORD *said to Noah, "Enter the ark, you and all your household, for you alone I have seen to be righteous before Me in this time."*   *—Genesis 7:1*

Noah's generation was perverse and deserved punishment. But Noah was a righteous man who walked with God and was granted protection. Noah proved his righteousness by obeying the Word of God in building the ark, gathering clean and unclean animals in pairs, and entering the ark (Genesis 7:5, 9, 11). The Lord closed the door behind Noah, preserving him and his family (7:16, 23). But the unrighteous were outside when the rain came and the waters rose and covered the mountain peaks—a terrible punishment. God is not finished judging the unrighteous and saving the righteous. Someday in the future, Christ's rapture of His church will come in the same manner as the flood in Noah's day—in a flash (Matthew 24:36–39). But then it will be too late for those on the outside. What are we doing *today* to invite others into the safety of eternal salvation?

Genesis 8

God remembered Noah and all the beasts and all the cattle that were with him in the ark; and God caused a wind to pass over the earth, and the water subsided.   *—Genesis 8:1*

Noah and his family were cooped up in a bobbing boat for forty days and nights. But after the torrential rains abated, God "remembered" the humans and animals He had saved by His grace. The Lord "caused a wind to pass over the earth," slowly revealing dry land until the ark came to rest on the peak of Ararat

(Genesis 8:1–5). Once the earth dried, the Lord commanded Noah to disembark and allow the animals to roam freely and repopulate the earth. After such a great deliverance from destruction, Noah built an altar and worshiped. This was fitting and pleasing to the Lord, who promised never again to "curse the ground" or "destroy every living thing" because of human evil (8:20–21) God continues to deliver His people from dangerous situations, providing protection and peace. When such protection comes our way, our first response should reflect Noah's—we ought to give thanks and praise.

Genesis 9

God blessed Noah and his sons and said to them, "Be fruitful and multiply, and fill the earth."   *—Genesis 9:1*

Lest anyone think that God holds life cheap or that taking life is a trivial matter, the Lord bound Himself to a promise to preserve life—signified by the rainbow—and bound humankind to a law that punished life-takers (Genesis 9:5–17). Both the covenant and the law were founded on the fact that human beings are made in the image of God, which demands that life be preserved (9:6). The *Imago Dei* also demands that human dignity be preserved—something Ham, unlike his brothers Shem and Japheth, failed to do when he discovered his father, Noah, lying naked in the tent (9:22–27). In today's culture of death and dishonor, life indeed is cheap. Christians must reject the ways of Ham and be like Shem and Japheth, whose reverence earned a blessing. Life is precious in the sight of God, and we, as God's image bearers, are responsible to protect and respect life—ours and others.

Genesis 10

These are the families of the sons of Noah, according to their genealogies, by their nations; and out of these the nations were separated on the earth after the flood. —Genesis 10:32

In what is known as The Table of Nations, Moses (the author of Genesis) highlighted three universal truths about humankind. First, the human race finds its origin in one family—the family of Noah (Genesis 10:1). Second, the human race is perpetually divided by language, race, territory, and politics (10:5, 20, 31). Third, the human race prospers under God's common blessing. The God who preserved Noah and his family and who sovereignly separated and blessed the various races of people is in control of all the nations on the earth—past, present, and future. This is a great comfort, especially when we hear news of wars, terrorism, and global recession. It often seems that the world is spinning out of control, but rest assured that God isn't absent, isn't surprised, and isn't powerless. When we turn on the news, we can remember this truth: "He rules over the nations" (Psalm 22:28)

Genesis 11

Its name was called Babel, because there the LORD confused the language of the whole earth; and from there the LORD scattered them abroad over the face of the whole earth. —Genesis 11:9

God commanded both Adam and Noah to "fill the earth" (Genesis 1:28; 9:1). But human hubris caused Noah's progeny to rebel against God and gather together in one place—on the plain of Shinar, where they built a city with a high tower. United by one language, the people of the earth joined together for security and social immortality. But the Lord was displeased. He confused their language, thereby fulfilling His original command (11:9). Out of all the families of the earth, God chose Shem, the forefather of Abram (Abraham), as a source of divine blessing to all peoples of the earth (11:10–32). The story of the Tower of Babel teaches us that those who exalt themselves God will abase and judge, but those who abase themselves God will exalt and bless. Our struggle is against pride's refusal to submit to God's authority. But humility is the only way to blessing.

Genesis 12

The LORD appeared to Abram and said, "To your descendants I will give this land." So he built an altar there to the LORD who had appeared to him. —*Genesis 12:7*

Abram's life was marked by faith and fear. When God called Abram to leave his homeland of Ur and promised to make him a great nation, Abram believed and obeyed. Promised the land of Canaan in perpetuity, Abram worshiped God in faith (Genesis 12:7). But when a famine struck and Abram and Sarai traveled to Egypt, Abram feared for his life, deceived Pharaoh, and allowed his wife to be put in Pharaoh's harem (12:12). Thankfully, the Lord rescued Sarai. Faith and fear are common to all who respond to the call of God. Faith prompts us to trust and obey God alone, and so we step out in response to God's leading. Fear, however, causes us to forget God and seek human solutions to life's difficulties, especially when God seems distant or confusing. When fear pushes out faith, we can remind ourselves of God's faithfulness and resist giving fear a foothold.

Genesis 13

Abram said to Lot, "Please let there be no strife between you and me . . . for we are brothers. Is not the whole land before you? Please separate from me; if to the left, then I will go to the right; or if to the right, then I will go to the left." —*Genesis 13:8–9*

After the Lord saved Sarai, Abram returned to Canaan, to the place where he first worshiped the Lord. However, a land dispute arose between Abram's herdsmen and Lot's herdsmen. Being assured of God's promise and wanting to avert family conflict, Abram magnanimously offered Lot his choice of grazing land. Lot chose the best of the land. Abram moved to Hebron. Because of Abram's faith and generosity, the Lord reaffirmed His covenant with Abram: wherever Abram's eye gazed or his foot trod would be his and his descendants' forever (Genesis 13:14–18). Abram's response to Lot teaches us that the life of faith is one of generosity. Generosity takes nothing away from us—even if it appears we've lost the best. The Lord knows how to provide for His own. And if we will only trust in Him and wait for His provision, we'll see that the best is in His hands.

Genesis 14

Abram said to the king of Sodom, "I have sworn to the LORD God Most High, possessor of heaven and earth, that I will not take a thread or a sandal thong or anything that is yours, for fear you would say, 'I have made Abram rich.'" —*Genesis 14:22–23*

This curious chapter seems to have little to do with Abram. But from the story of the warring kings, we can draw several observations and conclusions about Abram and God's promise to him. Abram was established in the land of promise. He protected his family and possessions by driving out the invading kings who took Lot captive. Abram was a powerful tribal leader—those who blessed him were blessed by God; those who didn't suffered defeat. Abram demonstrated faith by choosing to wait for God's blessing rather than accepting the spoils of war and placing himself in debt to a pagan king (Genesis 14:17–24). As it did for Abram, the world holds many alluring enticements and entertainments which might distract or discourage us from trusting God when life becomes difficult. But we can demonstrate faith like Abram by waiting on God and turning a blind eye to the world's spoils.

Genesis 15

And He took him outside and said, "Now look toward the heavens, and count the stars, if you are able to count them." And He said to him, "So shall your descendants be." Then he believed in the LORD; and He reckoned it to him as righteousness.   —Genesis 15:5–6

God promised to make Abram "a great nation" and multiply his reward (Genesis 12:2; 15:1). But Abram was childless. How would God fulfill His promise? Not through Eliezer, Abram's servant whom he considered adopting, but rather through Abram's own body. Abram's descendants would number as high as the stars in the sky. Abram believed God, and God blessed Abram. God repeated His promise regarding the land, and though a time would come when Abram's children would be strangers and slaves in a foreign land, the Lord would redeem them and bring them back to the land of promise (15:7–16). Life is filled with longings, perhaps for the salvation of a loved one, the cure of a disease, or the return of Jesus. The waiting sometimes seems a burden too heavy to bear. Yet, if we, like Abram, trust God, we'll experience God's will in God's time, even if the fulfillment of our desires is delayed.⟩

Genesis 16

So Hagar bore Abram a son; and Abram called the name of his son, whom Hagar bore, Ishmael.   *—Genesis 16:15*

The life of faith is not easy. It requires patience and persistence—two qualities lacking in the narrative of Genesis 16. Ten years had passed since God's initial promise to make Abram a great nation. Yet Sarai remained barren. She had waited long enough. According to custom, Sarai gave her maiden, Hagar, to Abram as a concubine in hopes of fulfilling God's promise (Genesis 16:2–3). In weakness, Abram agreed to the plan and impregnated Hagar. Then Hagar despised Sarai. Sarai despised Abram. Abram banished Hagar. And Hagar saw God. The lesson of faith is clear: those who are in need should call on the Lord, who hears and sees, and should wait for His provision. We shouldn't take action on our own in an impatient attempt to fulfill God's calling or God's promises. To use human means to accomplish what only God can do is to invite trouble—both now and in the future.

Genesis 17

Now when Abram was ninety-nine years old, the LORD appeared to Abram and said to him,
"I am God Almighty;
Walk before Me, and be blameless.
I will establish My covenant between Me and you,
And I will multiply you exceedingly."   *—Genesis 17:1–2*

It had been thirteen years since the Lord last spoke to Abram about the promise of making his descendants as numerous as the stars. The Lord once again came to Abram to reassure him that the divine promise was true. God's pledge was sealed by changing Abram's name to Abraham — "the father of many" — and changing Sarai's name to Sarah. But Abraham had to continue to live by faith — to walk blamelessly before the Lord — in obedience to God's commands (Genesis 17:2), starting with the command of circumcision (17:9–14). Likewise, we are to live before the Lord, blameless in word and deed (Deuteronomy 18:13; Matthew 5:48). This is impossible to accomplish on our own. The only surefire means of accomplishing such holiness is to submit to God's Spirit, spend time with God in His Word, and obey what it says.

Genesis 18

"Is anything too difficult for the LORD? At the appointed time I will return to you, at this time next year, and Sarah will have a son."

—*Genesis 18:14*

Nothing is impossible with God. And nothing escapes His notice. The Lord, accompanied by two angels, visited Abraham to announce that God was about to do the impossible: within a year, Sarah would deliver a son (Genesis 18:9–11). After the birth announcement, the Lord told Abraham He intended to destroy the cities of Sodom and Gomorrah. Abraham, however, interceded on behalf of the righteous in those cities, if any could be found. The Lord assured Abraham He would spare the cities if ten righteous people were found (18:22–33). This conversation teaches us that God can accomplish anything He determines to do, whether creating a life in the womb of an old woman or saving a city. With such a God, we should not fear life's present or future difficulties. And because God is willing to save the wicked (2 Peter 3:9), we must pray for the salvation of lost souls.

Genesis 19

The LORD rained on Sodom and Gomorrah brimstone and fire from the LORD out of heaven, and He overthrew those cities, and all the valley, and all the inhabitants of the cities, and what grew on the ground. —Genesis 19:24–25

The story of Sodom and Gomorrah is the story of destruction and deliverance. It's also the story of how God's people were pulled into a downward spiral of depravity. It's the story of a family who lived among the wicked, of a man who offered his daughters to a lustful mob, of a man who was reluctant to obey God's command and who negotiated with God, of a disobedient wife, and of a family reduced to incest to keep the family line going (so the daughters erroneously thought). In Lot, we see this truth in living color: passivity toward cultural sin leads to passivity toward personal sin. We must take special care, especially in our sex-saturated culture, to protect our eyes and minds and those of our children from ungodly influences and practices, lest we accept and practice similar sins. Paul was right: "Bad company corrupts good morals" (1 Corinthians 15:33).

Genesis 20

God came to Abimelech in a dream of the night, and said to him, "Behold, you are a dead man because of the woman whom you have taken, for she is married." —Genesis 20:3

Abraham and Sarah were up to their old tricks, but this time, it almost cost a man and his kingdom their lives. Though Abimelech's motive in taking Sarah into his harem was innocent enough, the fact remained: he *had* taken another man's wife — a violation of God's design for marriage and an issue of life-and-death. To make things right, Abimelech confessed his innocence and restored Sarah (Genesis 20:5, 14). But it wasn't until Abraham prayed for Abimelech that the Lord blessed Abimelech and all who were in his kingdom. The purity of marriage is a serious matter to the Lord, as this story illustrates. God's passion and firmness about the purity of marriage should prompt us to keep our own marriage beds undefiled (Hebrews 13:4). We must take this to heart as ever-increasing infidelity rates reach plague-like levels, not just among the general population but also among Christians.

Genesis 21

Then the LORD took note of Sarah as He had said, and the LORD did for Sarah as He had promised. So Sarah conceived and bore a son to Abraham in his old age, at the appointed time of which God had spoken to him. — Genesis 21:1–2

As promised, according to God's word, Sarah conceived and gave birth to a son, Isaac, who brought joy to her aged heart (Genesis 21:1–3). But, for Sarah, Ishmael was a threat to God's promise, so Sarah asked Abraham to cast out Ishmael and Hagar — which Abraham did. Once in the wilderness, Hagar and Ishmael suffered under the threat of death. However, the Lord heard Ishmael's cry for help, and God preserved their lives, promising to make Ishmael a great nation (21:15–21). God is a promise maker and a promise keeper. For Sarah it was the promise of a son. For Ishmael it was a promise of provision and prosperity. Though Christians today have no promise of prosperity from the Lord, we do have His promise of provision. He will take care of our daily needs. For this reason, just as Jesus said, we have no reason to worry, even if we are experiencing wilderness-like days (Matthew 6:25–33).

Genesis 22

Now it came about after these things, that God tested Abraham, and said to him, "Abraham! . . . Take now your son, your only son, whom you love, Isaac, and go to the land of Moriah, and offer him there as a burnt offering on one of the mountains of which I will tell you."

—*Genesis 22:1–2*

God tests His people to determine the quality of their faith. In times past, Abraham had been a faithful but fearful man. After the birth of Isaac, the son of promise, Abraham's fear of others turned into the fear of God—the mark of true faith. The test of that faith came when God called Abraham to sacrifice Isaac. Without hesitation, Abraham "rose early in the morning" and took Isaac to Mount Moriah, bound him, and raised the knife to thrust (Genesis 22:3–10). But God stopped him! As Abraham predicted, God provided a ram for the sacrifice and blessed Abraham (22:8, 11–19). The most difficult aspect of faith comes when God calls on us to sacrifice those things we most treasure. But if we have the faith of Abraham—a faith marked by the fear of God—we'll obediently sacrifice our wills, our dreams, and our hopes as an act of worship.

Genesis 23

Abraham buried Sarah his wife in the cave of the field at
Machpelah . . . in the land of Canaan. So the field and the cave that
is in it, were deeded over to Abraham for a burial site by the sons
of Heth.   *—Genesis 23:19–20*

God's promises never die, even if those who look for the fulfillment of those promises die. Sarah rejoiced in the son of
promise, Isaac, but she died before Isaac married and fathered
children—before she could see the fulfillment of God's promises (Genesis 23:1–2). But even in Sarah's death and burial, God
continued to bring about what He promised to Abraham—to
establish the land of Canaan as a perpetual possession. Abraham
had sojourned in Canaan, but in burying Sarah, he purchased
land (23:17–20). Death's curse cannot alter God's plans for His
people—for them to fellowship with Him and to be a source of
blessing to others. During our brief lives, we, like Sarah, have
the privilege of taking part in God's divine plan, knowing that
the fulfillment of God's promises are based on His character, His
power, and His timing, not ours.

Genesis 24

"Blessed be the Lord, the God of my master Abraham, who has not
forsaken His lovingkindness and His truth toward my master; as for
me, the Lord has guided me in the way to the house of my master's
brothers."   *—Genesis 24:27*

Faithfulness is a hallmark of God and of God's servants, and the
account of how Isaac acquired a wife is exemplary. Abraham, his
servant, and Rebekah each demonstrated faithfulness to God by
following His will: Abraham commissioned his servant to find

a bride for his son. The servant trusted the Lord to guide him as he carried out the commission, and he prioritized God's program over his own comforts (Genesis 24:27, 54–56). Rebekah believed that the servant's word was God's will for her life — that she should marry Isaac (24:58). In a world that seeks its own will, this narrative provides a much-needed corrective. For us, the tests of true faithfulness still include having a single-minded focus to discover God's will, giving God's will priority over our own desires and comforts, and trusting God to guide us as we seek to be obedient to His will.

Genesis 25

The LORD said to her,
"Two nations are in your womb;
And two peoples will be separated from your body;
And one people shall be stronger than the other;
And the older shall serve the younger."   — *Genesis 25:23*

Abraham didn't select the Lord; the Lord selected him and graciously blessed him. That divine blessing passed from Abraham to Isaac and, with the birth of Jacob and Esau, to God's elect — Jacob. The Lord's words to Rebekah had come to pass: "The older shall serve the younger" (Genesis 25:23). The first indication that God's Word was true concerning Jacob (the second born) and Esau (the first born) occurred when Esau despised his birthright and sold it to Jacob for a bowl of stew (25:27–34). Many people struggle with the notion of divine election, but God's selection of Jacob over Esau makes clear the importance of this doctrine. Just as Jacob, Isaac, and Abraham were chosen, God's children today are also elected by God's sovereign grace to receive the blessing of eternal life. The blessing of election, however, carries the responsibility of obedience and of blessing others by "proclaim[ing] the excellencies of [Christ]" (1 Peter 2:9).

Genesis 26

So Isaac lived in Gerar. When the men of the place asked about his wife, he said, "She is my sister," for he was afraid to say, "my wife," thinking, "the men of the place might kill me on account of Rebekah, for she is beautiful." —Genesis 26:6–7

Isaac was the son of his father, even to the point of demonstrating the same faith and fear. When a famine came, the Lord commanded Isaac to sojourn in Gerar, the land of the Philistines. There the Lord would bless him (Genesis 26:1–5). Isaac did so, but fearing for his life on account of Rebekah's beauty, told Abimelech that she was his sister. When Isaac's deception was discovered, Abimelech was angry. The king later drove Isaac out of Gerar because Isaac was growing too powerful for the king's comfort (26:6–17). Though the Lord continued to bless Isaac after he departed Gerar and settled in Beersheba, this story teaches us an important lesson about honesty and faithfulness. Life is filled with difficulties, with plenty of opportunities to deceive others in order to protect ourselves or to get our own way. But God's children must never resort to lies; rather, during difficult days, we ought to increase our trust in God.

Genesis 27

Then Isaac said to Jacob, "Please come close, that I may feel you, my son, whether you are really my son Esau or not." So Jacob came close to Isaac his father, and he felt him and said, "The voice is the voice of Jacob, but the hands are the hands of Esau."   *—Genesis 27:21–22*

God works out His will through and often despite sinful humans. But negative consequences always accompany sin. When it came time for Isaac to transfer the divine blessing, he knew it belonged to Jacob, yet he tried to thwart God's Word by blessing Esau. Esau, in agreeing to his father's plan, broke faith with Jacob concerning the birthright. Rebekah and Jacob, though they had the promise of God, went about fulfilling God's promise through trickery (Genesis 27:6–17). And though Jacob did receive the blessing, it came at a cost: hatred and separation within the family (27:40–46). Like Rebekah and Jacob, when we know God's will, we are often tempted to rush ahead and bring it to fruition on our own timetable. When we do that, we manipulate events and deceive others. The fallout often consists of broken relationships and damaged reputations.

Genesis 28

"I am the LORD, the God of your father Abraham and the God of Isaac; the land on which you lie, I will give it to you and to your descendants. . . . And in you and in your descendants shall all the families of the earth be blessed."   *—Genesis 28:13–14*

On the heels of deceiving his father and manipulating the blessing from his brother, Jacob fled to Paddan-aram to find a wife. Stopping for the night outside the gates of Luz, Jacob lay down and dreamed of God's angels ascending and descending on a ladder. Suddenly, the Lord appeared and blessed Jacob. When Jacob woke, he took his rock-pillow, constructed a pillar, and worshiped the Lord, renaming the city Bethel—the "House of God"—and pledging a perpetual tithe (Genesis 28:16–22). Today, the Lord no longer appears to His people in visions or speaks to them in an audible voice because we have His Word. But He continues to seek worshipers and gladly accepts their worship if done in "spirit and in truth" (John 4:23–24) And we have the privilege of worshiping God at any time—day or night, Monday through Sunday.

Genesis 29

And [Jacob] said to Laban, "What is this you have done to me? Was it not for Rachel that I served with you? Why then have you deceived me?" —Genesis 29:25

"Do not be deceived, God is not mocked; for whatever a man sows, this he will also reap" (Galatians 6:7) The principle of sowing and reaping is replete throughout Scripture, but no greater example is the life of Jacob—the deceiver who was deceived. By divine providence, Jacob reached Paddan-aram and met his future wife. Laban, Jacob's uncle, took him in, and Jacob worked seven years for the hand of Rachel, whom he loved. But when it came time for the wedding, Laban deceived Jacob and gave him Leah, the older sister (Genesis 29:21–26). For another seven years of work, Jacob was promised Rachel as well (29:27–30). The lesson? The consequences of sin may not bear immediate fruit, but if we are unwilling to root out sin from our lives, the Lord will bring in a rich harvest of discipline, just as Galatians 6:7 warns.

Genesis 30

Now when Rachel saw that she bore Jacob no children, she became
jealous of her sister; and she said to Jacob, "Give me children, or else
I die." —Genesis 30:1

The brewing feud between Leah and Rachel boiled over with the
birth of Leah's first child. Both women, in an effort to outdo each
other in the race to produce children, gave their handmaidens to
Jacob — and even went so far as to bargain for Jacob's affection
(Genesis 30:1–21). Eventually, barren and beloved Rachel conceived her own son, Joseph. After Joseph's birth, Jacob sought to
depart from Laban, who was reluctant to let him go. Jacob agreed
to remain and work for wages of sheep and goats. Jacob strengthened his flocks while Laban's flocks grew weak. Though God
blessed Jacob while he lived with and worked for Laban, Jacob's
family life was a source of constant strain. God's favor on our
professional lives isn't always accompanied with harmony in our
personal lives. This is especially true if our families function out
of jealousy or rivalry instead of mutual understanding and love.

Genesis 31

Jacob saw the attitude of Laban, and behold, it was not friendly
toward him as formerly. —Genesis 31:2

Twenty years — that's how long Jacob worked for his father-in-
law, Laban: seven years for Leah, seven years for Rachel, and
six years for wages. Now it was time to go, to return to the
Promised Land. So out of obedience to the call of God, Jacob
gathered his family and his flocks and quietly left Paddan-aram
(Genesis 31:1–21). Three days later, Laban hurried after Jacob,
catching him at Gilead. Though Laban and Jacob argued, they

parted in peace (31:43–55). God is interested not in our comfort but in growing us up. God's favorite methods to mature us include difficulties—hardships that chisel and file our character until we reflect the character of God. The years with Laban were difficult for Jacob, but his commitment to the maturing process is an example we all should follow. If we do, God will cause even our enemies to be a peace with us (Proverbs 16:7).

Genesis 32

"Your name shall no longer be Jacob, but Israel; for you have striven with God and with men and have prevailed." —*Genesis 32:28*

Twenty years of absence didn't cause Esau to forget his threat to kill his brother, Jacob (Genesis 27:41). Upon approaching Esau's stronghold, two angels met Jacob—a sign of God's protection (32:1–2). Nevertheless, Jacob sent gifts to assuage Esau's anger, because he feared Esau more than he trusted God. How often we are just like Jacob, allowing our fear to trump our faith. Often, before allowing the Lord to work on our behalf, we turn inward and rely on our self-sufficiency. But that's not God's way. God wrestled with Jacob, dislocated his hip, and changed his name to Israel, all for the sake of realigning his faith (32:22–32). Like Jacob we, too, may leave our time with God with scars—which are really divine blessings, reminders that we are weak and He is strong.

Genesis 33

"No, please, if now I have found favor in your sight, then take my present from my hand, for I see your face as one sees the face of God, and you have received me favorably."   *—Genesis 33:10*

God can soften the hardest of hearts. This is the story of Jacob and Esau's reunion at Peniel. However, as Esau arrived, Jacob anticipated revenge. In fear, he placed his least favored wives and children in the front, the place of potential danger, and kept his most favored wife and child in the back, the place of relative safety (Genesis 33:1–2). But Esau hadn't come for revenge; he had come for reconciliation. And what a beautiful reconciliation it was, complete with tears and gifts (33:3–11). This episode reminds us that strife and misunderstandings, whether within families or friendships or work relationships, are part of life. But strained or broken relationships need not remain so. Reconciliation is possible. When we take responsibility for our part, seek to forgive and be forgiven, and trust the Lord, He can repair even the greatest breaches.

Genesis 34

But they said, "Should he treat our sister as a harlot?"
    —Genesis 34:31

Zeal for justice sometimes leads to injustice. This was true concerning the rape of Dinah, Jacob's daughter, and the revenge taken on her behalf. When Shechem raped Dinah and sought to marry her, Jacob failed to act (Genesis 34:1–7). Dinah's brothers, however, did, and they used circumcision as part of their revenge (34:25–29). Though Dinah deserved justice, her brothers used that which was holy—the sign of God's covenant with

Abraham—to accomplish an unholy and unjust act—mass murder. Shechem was the guilty man, but in their quest for justice, Simeon and Levi inflicted injustice upon an entire community. Jacob's indifference and failure to demand justice for Dinah precipitated his sons' unjust acts. The principle for any leader, whether in the home, the church, the business world, or the realm of politics, is clear: when those in leadership fail to act decisively and wisely in the face of evil, the immature—in their zeal—may dishonor God by seeking justice unjustly.

Genesis 35

Then God said to Jacob, "Arise, go up to Bethel and live there, and make an altar there to God, who appeared to you when you fled from your brother Esau." So Jacob said to his household and to all who were with him, "Put away the foreign gods which are among you."
—Genesis 35:1–2

Spiritual complacency creeps in when we get comfortable. When Jacob saw the heavenly vision at Bethel, he made a vow to God (Genesis 28:20–22). But years passed and Jacob still hadn't fulfilled it. So the Lord reminded Jacob to return to Bethel (Genesis 35:1). Before the journey, the family members recommitted themselves to the Lord by throwing away their idols. In Bethel, God renewed His covenant with Jacob, and Jacob worshiped (35:2–15). Jacob had lived many hard years under Laban, but God had blessed Jacob. And though other joys and sorrows came, prosperity had caused the family to become spiritually lazy and cozy with idol worship. Something similar often happens to Christians during certain seasons of life. Ease can cause complacency to crawl into our spiritual lives, making us so comfortable with sin that we forget our vow to worship God alone.

Genesis 36

Then Esau took his wives and his sons and his daughters and all his household, and his livestock and all his cattle and all his goods which he had acquired in the land of Canaan, and went to another land away from his brother Jacob. — *Genesis 36:6*

God blessed Esau; he became the father of many and grew wealthy and powerful in the hill country of Seir (Genesis 36:1–8). Esau's success may seem like an oddity, since the Bible portrays him as a fleshly man, not a spiritual man (Hebrews 12:16). Because Jacob merely sojourned in Canaan (Genesis 37:1) while Esau possessed land as the head of a vast dynasty, it would seem God's greater blessing was on Esau, not Jacob — the son of promise. But the narrative of Esau's riches and power is an apt illustration of an often forgotten spiritual truth: secular greatness grows rapidly, while spiritual greatness grows slowly. The Bible records the character of both men. We despise the one for his irreverence and praise the other for his faith. The lesson for us? If we are to establish praiseworthy character, we must remain faithful and persevere, even if others bask in worldly success.

Genesis 37

"Now then, come and let us kill him and throw him into one of the pits; and we will say, 'A wild beast devoured him.' Then let us see what will become of his dreams!" — *Genesis 37:20*

From the beginning, Joseph was his father's favorite — the son of Jacob's old age and of Jacob's beloved Rachel. But Joseph was also favored because he was faithful and righteous, unlike his brothers. Jacob determined that Joseph would receive the blessing — a choice confirmed by God, who gave Joseph divine dreams and their interpretations (Genesis 37:5–11). The envious brothers hated Joseph and plotted to kill him, but they settled instead on selling Joseph to an Egypt-bound caravan (37:19–28). The brothers' reaction to God's choice is like a boney finger poking us in the sternum. When we are passed over for a promotion or fail to win the praise of those we respect, our natural reaction is to express jealousy or hatred. But when jealousy creeps into our souls, we should confess and resist revenge, remembering God's ways are higher than our ways. In contentment we can learn to rejoice in God's choice.

Genesis 38

"I am with child by the man to whom these things belong." And she said, "Please examine these and see, whose signet ring and cords and staff are these?" Judah recognized them, and said, "She is more righteous than I, inasmuch as I did not give her to my son Shelah."
— *Genesis 38:25–26*

God's activities are often ironic and corrective. Judah, a son of promise, was an unfaithful son by failing to keep the fulfillment of the promise within the family. He married a Canaanite woman, showed indifference toward his daughter-in-law's legal right to bear children within the family, and committed an immoral act with Tamar. He then proved he was a hypocrite by threatening to punish Tamar for her harlotry while failing to address his own sin. Ironically, Tamar, though not a daughter of promise, proved more righteous in the eyes of God than Judah (Genesis 38:26–30). This episode teaches that being a Christian doesn't guarantee that a person will live like God's child. It also teaches that those who aren't God's children may at times prove more righteous than those who are. The irony, then, is that we should follow Tamar's example as opposed to Judah's. Though Judah was a son of promise, Tamar followed God's plan, while Judah pursued self-gratification and found himself corrected by God.

Genesis 39

"There is no one greater in this house than I, and he has withheld nothing from me except you, because you are his wife. How then could I do this great evil and sin against God?" — Genesis 39:9

Temptations always threaten to derail God's children from fulfilling their callings. For Joseph, whom God blessed, giving in to the temptation to gratify himself with a willing mistress would have invalidated his potential as God's chosen leader. Joseph knew that such sexual immorality was a sin against God, not just against Potiphar (Genesis 39:1–9). Joseph would rather have been falsely accused of rape and thrown into prison than allow his sin to stain God's reputation among a pagan people and nullify his influence as God's representative among them. Like Joseph, we do not live in a godly culture. Like Joseph, we represent God to people who know nothing of Him. That's why our moral purity is so vital. Few sins are more destructive to our witness than sexual immorality. But a firm dedication to God's calling as His representatives on earth is a powerful inducement to resist temptation.

Genesis 40

Yet the chief cupbearer did not remember Joseph, but forgot him. — Genesis 40:23

In Potiphar's house, Joseph passed the purity test. In prison, he faced another: the faith test. The exam came in the form of a dream-interpretation sequence. Joseph passed this test when he testified that interpretations belong to God and when the interpretation Joseph offered came true. However, just because Joseph made an A+ on the faith test didn't mean the Lord was through with him. Joseph also had to pass the patience test; the cupbearer's neglect meant Joseph would remain in prison indefinitely. For many people, the patience test is the hardest exam of all. God often waits to promote His people to the next level of responsibility until after He has tested their faith in His promises, and such tests often involve discouraging situations during periods of waiting. It's the few who remain faithful and patient, particularly when life seems unfair, who prove their spiritual maturity and their readiness for God's next assignment.

Genesis 41

So Pharaoh said to Joseph, "Since God has informed you of all this, there is no one so discerning and wise as you are. You shall be over my house, and according to your command all my people shall do homage; only in the throne I will be greater than you."

—*Genesis 41:39–40*

Joseph spent two additional years in prison after interpreting the cupbearer's dream (Genesis 41:1). And it wasn't until Pharaoh's dreams stumped the wise men of Egypt that Joseph was freed. As before, Joseph boldly credited God with dream interpretation. Joseph hadn't grown cold or cynical toward God in the dungeon; rather Joseph remembered God's power and faithfulness. Joseph told Pharaoh of seven coming years of plenty followed by seven years of famine and outlined a plan of provision. Pharaoh promoted Joseph to prime minister (41:37–45), and Egypt survived the famine. The rewards of faithfulness rarely come quickly or easily. But if we maintain a spirit of humility and dependence on God, as Joseph did, then God can use us to impact homes, neighborhoods, states, and in some cases, whole nations. God still looks for those whose hearts are fully devoted to Him. Such hearts might change the culture, even in our day.

Genesis 42

Then they said to one another, "Truly we are guilty concerning our brother, because we saw the distress of his soul when he pleaded with us, yet we would not listen; therefore this distress has come upon us."
— *Genesis 42:21*

God is not in the business of blessing His wayward children; rather, He is in the business of bringing them to a point of blessing . . . through discipline. Suffering under the famine, Joseph's brothers journeyed to Egypt and stood before him to buy grain . . . and Joseph remembered his teenaged dreams (Genesis 42:1–9). Accusing them of spying, Joseph incarcerated his brothers. After three days, Joseph released all but Simeon, telling the brothers not to return unless they brought Benjamin with them. Joseph's test accomplished its desired result: the brothers finally acknowledged their sin (42:21–22). In the same way today, God will not let the consciences of the faithful rest until we deal with unresolved sin. And if He must use severe trials to break through our sin-hardened hearts, He will.

Genesis 43

He took portions to them from his own table, but Benjamin's portion was five times as much as any of theirs. So they feasted and drank freely with him.
— *Genesis 43:34*

The family ran out of food . . . again. The brothers needed to return to Egypt, but they dared not do so without Benjamin. Finally, Jacob allowed it, and sent them on their way with gifts and money. When they arrived in Egypt, Joseph hosted a banquet for his brothers, who had finally shown responsibility, honesty, and unity. But Joseph desired to test them again. Would they be jealous when he showed favoritism to Benjamin? Joseph lavished five times as much food on Benjamin's plate, and the brothers expressed gratitude instead of jealousy (Genesis 43:34). Spiritual maturity is always revealed in the flesh and blood of relationships—in how we treat others. In this regard, we should follow the example of Joseph's brothers, thinking of others before ourselves, caring for their needs, and accepting our lot with gratitude, even if others are elevated above us.

Genesis 44

"Now, therefore, please let your servant remain instead of the lad a slave to my lord, and let the lad go up with his brothers."

—*Genesis 44:33*

Joseph tested his brothers' consciences in chapter 43. In chapter 44, he tested their loyalty. Joseph had their money returned to them and a silver cup placed in Benjamin's sack. After the brothers departed, Joseph's steward caught up with them and performed a search. The one with the cup was to become Joseph's slave—and the cup was found in Benjamin's sack (Genesis 44:12–13). Though Joseph accused the brothers of doing something of which they were innocent (spying) and accused Benjamin of doing something of which he was innocent (stealing), Judah confessed their true guilt (slave trading) and offered himself in Benjamin's place (44:16, 33–34). Judah's heroics represent a foreshadowing of Christ's act on the cross and a shining example of what God expects all His children to do—lay down our lives for others as an act of self-sacrificial love and loyalty, motivated by a clean conscience (John 15:13; 1 John 3:16).

Genesis 45

"Now do not be grieved or angry with yourselves, because you sold me here, for God sent me before you to preserve life. . . . Now, therefore, it was not you who sent me here, but God." —*Genesis 45:5, 8*

Unable to control himself any longer, Joseph revealed his true identity, much to the astonishment of his brothers (Genesis 45:1–3). Joseph forgave them, because he saw in their evil deed God's providence. Joseph told them to retrieve their father and their families and bring them to Egypt to live in peace. This episode in Joseph's relationship with his brothers teaches that a divine perspective on life makes forgiveness and reconciliation possible. Few can cut us deeper than family. If we keep our eyes only on our wounds, they'll fester and become infected, threatening to sever our most precious relationships. But if we look to the Great Physician, He will bind up our wounds and make a way for forgiveness. And where there's forgiveness, there's the possibility of reconciliation and restoration of harmony in the family. So, we should ask: "What family offense do I need to ask for forgiveness?" or "What family offense do I need to forgive?"

Genesis 46

"I am God, the God of your father; do not be afraid to go down to Egypt, for I will make you a great nation there. I will go down with you to Egypt, and I will also surely bring you up again; and Joseph will close your eyes." —*Genesis 46:3–4*

Jacob spent twenty years outside the land of promise while working for Laban. And once Jacob made it back into the land, he planned on dying there. But God had different plans. Jacob and his family would sojourn in Egypt, and the patriarch would die in that foreign land. But Jacob (Israel) received this promise from God: He would remember His covenant (Genesis 46:2–4). Joseph would take care of Jacob, and he would prosper. When father and son reunited after twenty-two years, both wept a long time (46:29). Jacob's life is a roadmap of what it's like to walk with God—hopes and disappointments, obedience and disobedience, faith and fears. God is never finished maturing us on our journey of faith, taking us down roads that twist and turn. But we can be "confident of this very thing, that He who began a good work in [us] will perfect it" (Philippians 1:6).

Genesis 47

Then Joseph said to the people, "Behold, I have today bought you and your land for Pharaoh; now, here is seed for you, and you may sow the land. At the harvest you shall give a fifth to Pharaoh, and four-fifths shall be your own for seed of the field and for your food and for those of your households and as food for your little ones."

—*Genesis 47:23–24*

God promised to make Abraham a great nation and to bless those who blessed him (Genesis 12:2–3). This promise came true in Egypt during the days of Joseph. Joseph moved his family to Egypt and, at the command of Pharaoh, gave them the best land where they then prospered (47:27). Such a blessing on God's people brought blessings upon Egypt, as Joseph administered the affairs of state with wisdom—saving the lives of many, prospering Pharaoh, and glorifying God (47:13–26). The principle for people of faith today is simple: we must work with wisdom and diligence, seeking to bless others, our employers, and our God. To accomplish this, we must keep in mind that, ultimately, we do not work for others or for ourselves. Rather, we work for the Lord. We may earn our paychecks from our employers, but God is the One who ultimately rewards us (Colossians 3:22–24).

Genesis 48

He blessed them that day, saying,
"By you Israel will pronounce blessing, saying,
'May God make you like Ephraim and Manasseh!'"
Thus he put Ephraim before Manasseh.   — *Genesis 48:20*

As his father Jacob's (Israel's) days drew to a close, Joseph brought his two sons home to be blessed (Genesis 48:1). Seeing Joseph's sons, Jacob blessed them—setting the younger, Ephraim, over the older, Manasseh. Though Joseph was displeased, Jacob explained that the blessing was appropriate, just as it was appropriate that Joseph have "one portion more" than his brothers (48:8–22). Looking over Jacob's long life, the writer to the Hebrews selected the blessing of Ephraim and Manasseh as the epitome of the patriarch's faith (Hebrews 11:21). Why? Because faith that has been matured by a lifetime of experiences with God can discern the will of God. Even today, God longs for us to know His will, just as much as we long to discover it. Through time spent with God in prayer, in His Word, and with His people, we can come to discern the still, small voice of the Holy Spirit.

Genesis 49

All these are the twelve tribes of Israel, and this is what their father said to them when he blessed them. He blessed them, every one with the blessing appropriate to him. —Genesis 49:28

Nearing death, Jacob gathered his sons to "bless" them (Genesis 49:1–2). Because of his presumption, Reuben lost the right to rule. Simeon and Levi would be scattered because of their fierce anger. Judah would rule and abound because of his praise-worthy actions. Zebulun would dwell by the sea, and Issachar, because he loved ease, would become a slave. Dan would judge the people. Gad would be raided and have to fight for his rights. Asher would provide delicacies to royalty. Naphtali would speak words of victory. Joseph would receive a double portion and the protection of God. And Benjamin would share his wealth. This episode reminds us that though we cannot predict the future, our actions and natures can determine our children's destinies. Whether inherited through DNA or absorbed through day-to-day life, who we are as parents turns up in our children. Moreover, they will carry into adulthood the virtues and priorities we instill today through our words and our deeds.

Genesis 50

"Do not be afraid, for am I in God's place? As for you, you meant evil against me, but God meant it for good in order to bring about this present result, to preserve many people alive." —Genesis 50:19–20

After Jacob's death, the brothers feared Joseph would retaliate against them, so they sent a messenger to beg forgiveness (Genesis 50:15–18). Joseph told them not to fear; judgment was in God's hands. And though the intent behind the brothers' selling Joseph into slavery was evil, God turned it for good, using it to save many (Genesis 50:19–20). Before Joseph's death, he prophesied that his brothers' children would return to Canaan, thereby fulfilling God's covenant promise (50:24). Though God's children grew into a great nation in Egypt, that pagan land was not their home. We Christians find ourselves in a foreign, pagan land as well. This fallen world isn't our home. We are merely "aliens and strangers" here (1 Peter 2:11). A day will come, however, when we will experience an "exodus" and live in the "promise land" of heaven. Until then, we continue to sojourn, with faith and hope, amidst sin and death.

Chorus: "This World Is Not My Home". -
   I'm just a-passing thru
My treasures are laid up, somewhere beyond
   the blue
The angels beckon me from heaven's open door,
And I can't feel at home in this
   world any more,
O Lord, you know I have no friend
   like you . us

Exodus

Exodus 1

But the midwives feared God, and did not do as the king of Egypt had commanded them, but let the boys live. — *Exodus 1:17*

Living under the tyrannical rule of Pharaoh, the Hebrews faced the certain death of their sons—an effort by the Egyptian king to control the quickly swelling population of God's people. However, the Hebrew midwives delivering those sons respected the authority of God more than that of Pharaoh, a loyalty that led them to protect the lives of the newborns in their care. The midwives even went so far as to lie to Pharaoh, telling him the Hebrew women gave birth before a midwife could arrive (Exodus 1:19). Faithfulness in serving God leads us to align our priorities with His. He desires that we value life instead of death, that we offer the helpless shelter in the face of evil aggressors (Psalm 41:1; Isaiah 25:4). In a world that increasingly courts death, a decision for life can be as counter-cultural and refreshing as the decision the Hebrew midwives made in Egypt thousands of years ago.

Exodus 2

So he looked this way and that, and when he saw there was no one around, he struck down the Egyptian and hid him in the sand.

— *Exodus 2:12*

One day as he walked among his own people, Moses stumbled upon an Egyptian beating a Hebrew. The future leader of God's people made sure no one was watching and proceeded to commit murder, saving the poor Hebrew worker from further abuse. As is the case for many who sin, Moses believed his sin to be secret, known only to the Hebrew victim he had saved. And, as is also often the case, what the sinner thought was buried in secrecy eventually bubbled to the surface (Exodus 2:13–15). Moses's response when he found out others knew about his sin? He was fearful, just as we are when our carefully controlled illusion of goodness breaks down. Moses illustrates for us the futility of hiding our sin. What we shroud in darkness will always, ultimately, come into the light.

Exodus 3

And He said, "Certainly I will be with you, and this shall be the sign to you that it is I who have sent you: when you have brought the people out of Egypt, you shall worship God at this mountain."

—*Exodus 3:12*

We often misunderstand the nature of living in faith. Many times, particularly during days of suffering, we become overburdened by its difficulty, only seeing the steep road ahead. In these times, we can lose our conviction that God is with us. When Moses wandered the desert and God appeared to him in a burning bush, the Lord assured the shepherd of His presence. And God promised to be there when Moses went to Pharaoh on God's mission. But how would Moses really know that God was with him? God assured Moses by offering him a sign—a sign that would not come to pass until *after* Moses had completed his task of leading the people out of Egypt. God's response to Moses at the bush was little more than, "Trust Me." God often operates with His people in this way, assuring us of His faithfulness, while insisting we follow in trust—no matter how difficult the circumstances.

Exodus 4

*Then Moses said to the LORD, "Please, Lord, I have never been elo-
quent, neither recently nor in time past, nor since You have spoken to
Your servant; for I am slow of speech and slow of tongue."*

—Exodus 4:10

Moses had just received a startling revelation from God, an
encounter unlike any other in the pages of Scripture. God's
purpose? He wanted Moses to deliver a message to Pharaoh:
Let Israel go. Though Moses had witnessed no less than three
miracles during this short communication, he still felt he wasn't
up to the task (Exodus 3:2; 4:3, 6 –7). His feelings of inadequacy
led him to push back against God's clear revelation. We, like
Moses, often feel inadequate to the tasks before us, even to the
point of resisting God's clear direction. How often have we sighed
in defeat at the God-ordained path before us? Are we starting
from a position all that different from the one Moses did in this
account? When we obey God as Moses did, the Lord will provide
a way for us to be the people He desires.

Exodus 5

*But Pharaoh said, "Who is the LORD that I should obey His voice
to let Israel go? I do not know the LORD, and besides, I will not let
Israel go."*   *—Exodus 5:2*

Would you redirect your life based on the advice of someone
you didn't know? Could a stranger convince you, with a brief
command, to give up a life of goodness for one of cruelty?
Of course not. Is it any surprise then that Pharaoh responded
negatively when Moses brought him a command — not just a
piece of advice — from Yahweh, the Lord of heaven and earth?

Knowing Yahweh as the one true God, as Christians know Him, implies submissive action on our part. However, we should not wonder at — or worse, judge — the hard hearts of those who do not know Him (1 Corinthians 5:12). Pharaoh's self-sufficient actions, much like the misdirected deeds of the unbeliever today, are tragic and, sadly, expected. In light of that truth, let us leave judgment to God and instead pray for unbelievers to turn from their ways and adopt the path to life that God has opened for them.

Exodus 6

So Moses spoke thus to the sons of Israel, but they did not listen to Moses on account of their despondency and cruel bondage.

—*Exodus 6:9*

In contrast to Pharaoh, the sons of Israel knew better. They knew Yahweh — both from the traditions handed down by their fathers and from the testimony of Moses. And yet, despite this wealth of special knowledge, the people of Israel allowed their circumstances to guide them. Despondency and slavery led them to reject Moses, even wishing judgment upon their leader for breaching their relationship with Pharaoh (Exodus 5:21). One might expect God's response to have been judgment — the people knew better; therefore, they should have been punished. But instead of judgment, God offered grace. He commanded Moses to approach Pharaoh with the goal of redeeming the Hebrews from slavery (6:12–13). To the degree we follow Israel in their refusal to listen to God, we put God's grace to the test. Let us remember the Bible's admonition to turn our backs on sin and live as "instruments of righteousness" (Romans 6:12–13).

Exodus 7

Moses was eighty years old and Aaron eighty-three, when they spoke to Pharaoh. — *Exodus 7:7*

After Pharaoh had spoken against releasing the Hebrews (Exodus 5:2), the Lord sent Moses and Aaron back to the Egyptian leader (7:1–2). This time, along with the divine demand for release, they carried with them a miracle and a judgment. In this narrative, God deemed it significant to reveal the ages of His two servants: eighty and eighty-three — older men by all accounts. Clearly, God doesn't concern Himself with age as a (dis)qualification for His service. Paul made a similar point regarding the youth of Timothy (1 Timothy 4:12). How often do we allow age to dictate whether or not we or others have the capability to serve? Do we ignore or avoid the old or the young, believing them unable to relate or understand due to a difference from us in age? Young, old, or somewhere in between, we all have the potential to serve God and His people.

Exodus 8

But Pharaoh hardened his heart this time also, and he did not let the people go. — *Exodus 8:32*

Due to his unbelief, Pharaoh suffered from a major malady: a hard heart. Persuading Pharaoh to do something he had no interest in doing was nigh impossible. Moses and Aaron, speaking on behalf of the God of the universe, returned day after day, absorbing refusal after refusal, trying to get Pharaoh to let the people go. As Pharaoh's refusals piled up, he and his people suffered greater and greater hardships. Pharaoh's disobedience teaches us all an invaluable lesson: those who mean to walk with God need tender hearts. Faithfulness to the Lord demands flexibility and humility, the giving up of our own desires that we might embrace God's. Pharaoh knew nothing of these virtues, for he did not know Yahweh in faith, and the consequences eventually yielded death. When believers embrace the Lord, He will provide the tender hearts, and we will find ourselves on our way down the path that yields life.

Exodus 9

"But, indeed, for this reason I have allowed you to remain, in order to show you My power and in order to proclaim My name through all the earth." — *Exodus 9:16*

God always acts in accordance with His character and purposes. One of those purposes made clear throughout the Bible is His desire to make Himself known—to believers and unbelievers alike. We see this purpose carried out during the time of Moses, especially through the plagues that God sent upon the Egyptians and their land. God attributed the continued existence of Egypt—a pagan nation—to His purpose of making known His power to Egypt and His name throughout the earth. God saw the plagues, then, not simply as a means to persuade Pharaoh to let the people go, but also as an opportunity to display His power to an unbelieving people and spread His fame through the earth. While we often wonder at God's purpose in this circumstance or that, we need never doubt that He is making Himself known to us, through both the good and the bad.

Exodus 10

*Then [Pharaoh] said to them, "Thus may the L*ORD *be with you, if ever I let you and your little ones go! Take heed, for evil is in your mind."* —Exodus 10:10

Denying God leads to confusion over the most fundamental questions of life, including the difference between good and evil. Upon hearing the threat of the seventh plague — the locusts that would cover Egypt — Pharaoh refused to let the people go. He also believed Moses and Aaron had "evil" in their minds, as evidenced by their request for all the Hebrews to be let go. Pharaoh felt that the Hebrews should serve their God on Pharaoh's terms (Exodus 10:11). And in Pharaoh's world, only Pharaoh determined the line between good and evil. As he changed, so did the nature of good and evil. This kind of moral confusion, so clear in the leader of Egypt, continues today as we place our own desires above God's. Unless the Lord tethers us to the truth, we are doomed to be the final arbiters in distinguishing good from evil — a plan sure to end in ruin, just as it did for Pharaoh.

Exodus 11

"'Moreover, there shall be a great cry in all the land of Egypt, such as there has not been before and such as there shall never be again.'" —Exodus 11:6

The disobedience of one person impacts the lives of many. Romans tells us that this has been the case since the days of Adam (Romans 5:19), while this passage in Exodus illustrates the results in the lives of everyday people — the nameless Egyptians. Pharaoh, due to his significant position of power, had a wider circle of influence than most of us. But his sin worked in the same way our sin does: the consequences spread. He rejected the direct command of God. As a result, he suffered, and so did his people. Likewise when we reject the direct commands of God, we bring suffering, not just on our own heads, but on those of spouses, children, friends, and church members. In each cry of suffering that results from our sin, we can hear an echo of the cry that went out in Egypt that first, fateful Passover night.

Exodus 12

"And when your children say to you, 'What does this rite mean to you?' you shall say, 'It is a Passover sacrifice to the LORD who passed over the houses of the sons of Israel in Egypt when He smote the Egyptians, but spared our homes.'" And the people bowed low and worshiped. —*Exodus 12:26–27*

Our God has wrought great deeds in history. In Him, people have found salvation from earthly threats and redemption from spiritual bondage. Handed down to us through Scripture, the stories of God's dealings with His people drive our impulse to worship. Just prior to the night of the first Passover, the people worshiped, and they did so in advance of God's sparing them from certain death (Exodus 12:23). But God directed them to do more. They were to remember His releasing them from bondage under the protection of shed blood and to pass down to their children and their children's children the rite of Passover as a memorial of God's deliverance. We, like the Israelites, can bow in worship because of what God has done for His people. The old stories of the Davids, the Elijahs, and the Jeremiahs lead us to worship our faithful God. Most of all, we thank Him for our deliverance from bondage through the shed blood of His Son, Jesus.

Exodus 13

*The LORD was going before them in a pillar of cloud by day to lead
them on the way, and in a pillar of fire by night to give them light,
that they might travel by day and by night. He did not take away the
pillar of cloud by day, nor the pillar of fire by night, from before the
people.*   *—Exodus 13:21–22*

Once the Hebrews broke free from the Egyptians, God came to
His people in unique and tangible fashion. A pillar of cloud by
day and a pillar of fire by night led them toward a land that
promised freedom and abundance. In the early moments of
their release, adrenalin, joy, and anticipation fueled their travels.
But in the darker days to follow — beginning with the pursuit
by Pharaoh (Exodus 14) — they leaned on their visibly-present
God. What was true for the Hebrews more than three thousand
years ago remains true for us today: God always provides just
what we need. We can most easily perceive that reality when the
comforts of life have been replaced with trials and tribulations.
Sometimes He comes in the tangible care offered by another person; at others, He gives an inner peace or confidence. But we can
always trust that in our time of need, the Lord will draw near.

Exodus 14

"The LORD will fight for you while you keep silent."   *—Exodus 14:14*

With the Egyptians at their backs and the open sea before them,
the Israelites were out of options. Without adequate military
force to defend themselves against the mighty Egyptian army,
God's people had reached a dead end. And God had led them
there. The Lord had His reasons. Danger and desperation

provide opportunity for devotion and dependence. A hopeless people found reason for hope in the miraculous working of God, who in His grace, resurrected their hopes as only He could. The Lord parted the waters, led the Israelites through, and destroyed the Egyptian armies behind them (Exodus 14:21–30). God led Israel to that dead end to give them the proper fear and faith He required of His people. And He does the same for us today, leading us to places of desperation, where only He can work, so our faith in Him might be tried and strengthened.

Exodus 15

Moses and the sons of Israel sang this song to the LORD, and said,
"I will sing to the LORD, for He is highly exalted;
The horse and its rider He has hurled into the sea."   *—Exodus 15:1*

The news reminds us every day that something is wrong—some people in our world seem hell-bent on destruction . . . their own and others'. This has been true throughout the history of humanity. The Pharaoh of the Exodus watched his country suffer ten devastating plagues, the last of which took the lives of all the firstborn in Egypt (Exodus 12:29–30). And still, Pharaoh resisted the will of God by chasing the Hebrews down to the banks of the Red Sea. When God allowed His people to pass through the sea unharmed, the Lord closed the path on the Egyptian army, drowning them all. The song that God's people sang in the aftermath of this remarkable event praises God, exalting Him for delivering them. Though we feel conflicted about the fate of those who, like the Egyptians, do evil, we too must confess the hard truth that part of making the world right involves bringing some people low.

Exodus 16

"In the morning you will see the glory of the LORD, for He hears your grumblings against the LORD; and what are we, that you grumble against us?" —*Exodus 16:7*

We have all been disappointed in a leader. For many of us, that disappointment morphs into grumbling—we'll tell anyone who'll listen about the troubles caused by the man or woman in charge. After the Hebrews passed through the Red Sea, God's pillars of cloud and fire led them into a place called the wilderness of Sin. Finding no easy access to food, the people "grumbled against Moses and Aaron" (Exodus 16:2). God had visibly led them to this wilderness, yet the short-sighted people laid the blame at the feet of Moses and his brother. The words of Moses and Aaron in response to the grumbling make clear its truly destructive nature: in blaming their leaders, the people were actually complaining against the Lord. When we grumble against a faithful spiritual leader, we call God into question, bringing dissension not just into the church, but into our relationships with God as well.

Exodus 17

He named the place Massah and Meribah because of the quarrel of the sons of Israel, and because they tested the LORD, saying, "Is this the LORD among us, or not?" —*Exodus 17:7*

Moving through the desert beyond the Red Sea, the people once again questioned God's leadership, this time due to a lack of water (Exodus 17:3; see also Exodus 16:2). In just a few months, the people had watched plagues decimate their Egyptian captors, passed through the Red Sea on dry land, and received manna and quail daily. Now, in the first moments of a water shortage, Israel had the gall to question whether the Lord was among them. Don't we do the same thing? Ignoring the obvious and abundant signs of God's blessing in our lives, we focus on our lack. And because of our weakness and our self-centeredness, a deficit in one area implies to us that God has removed His presence from our lives. But as God made clear to the Israelites when He provided them water, He is always present and able to meet the needs of His people.

Exodus 18

Moses' father-in-law said to him, "The thing that you are doing is not good. You will surely wear out, both yourself and these people who are with you, for the task is too heavy for you; you cannot do it alone."
                                                        —Exodus 18:17–18

Everybody needs somebody. This is true in our professional lives and our personal lives, and it is no less true in our spiritual lives. The very act of trusting God for salvation is a recognition of need on our part. We need someone else—Jesus—to save us from ourselves. Moses's father-in-law, Jethro, understood the need for others. A man of long experience in the world, Jethro saw his son-in-law's workload on behalf of God's people and knew immediately that Moses needed to make changes (Exodus 18:14). Otherwise, Moses would end up with a load too heavy to bear. So Jethro suggested Moses enlist the able assistance of other wise men who could help him with his work. No matter the area of life, the Bible affirms our need for help and our responsibility to bear one another's burdens as we all pursue God's design for our lives.

Exodus 19

"'And you shall be to Me a kingdom of priests and a holy nation.'
These are the words that you shall speak to the sons of Israel."
—Exodus 19:6

Many believers wonder about their purpose in this world. While not the only answer the Bible provides to this question, Exodus 19:6—echoed in 1 Peter 2:9—provides direction for the uncertain believer. In the wilderness, the Hebrews needed a new direction, not just geographically, but spiritually. When the Lord established a two-fold identity for His people—a kingdom of priests and a holy nation—they better understood their role in the world. God expected His people to mediate His grace to the other nations of the earth and for Israel to do so as a nation set apart in devotion to Him. In the same way, God expects believers today to be emissaries of His grace in the world, a people set apart for works of righteousness. These pursuits should characterize our dealings with others and our understanding of ourselves as believers in a world desperate for goodness and grace.

Exodus 20

"I am the LORD your God, who brought you out of the land of Egypt,
out of the house of slavery."   *—Exodus 20:2*

Our interactions with others change dramatically when we live with confidence. But where does our confidence come from? The Lord's statement introducing the Ten Commandments establishes His people's confidence in Him. Using His name—Yahweh—to bookend the movement from bondage to freedom (Exodus 6:2; 20:2), God announced His presence in all facets of life. The Lord also invoked those decisive events that delivered the people from the hand of Pharaoh. God had proven, through His deeds, that He was sovereign over all. With the Lord bringing His will to pass in the world, God's people need not worry or wonder about the future. Each of God's people needs that assurance that derives only from Him. Confidence in God's good plan to release His people from spiritual bondage and deliver us to freedom spurs us to act with boldness and strength in the face of difficult circumstances.

Exodus 21

"If [a female slave] is displeasing in the eyes of her master who designated her for himself, then he shall let her be redeemed. . . . If he takes to himself another woman, he may not reduce her food, her clothing, or her conjugal rights." —Exodus 21:8, 10

Reading biblical accounts about slavery that do not speak against the practice can be confusing to the modern ear. The ancient world, however, was much different from our own. The people knew nothing of life without slavery. It was practiced by people all over the known world and even entered into voluntarily by some who had particular needs for security or stability. When the Lord spoke about the practice in Exodus 21:7–11, He clearly had the protection of the vulnerable in mind. Women were especially at risk in the ancient world, so God's directions in this passage regarding provision for female slaves and even circumstances that would bring them freedom make it clear that He wanted to protect a defenseless population. Believers today should still make a point to protect the defenseless and the vulnerable from the cruel, the unfeeling, and the greedy.

Exodus 22

"For every breach of trust, whether it is for ox, for donkey, for sheep, for clothing, or for any lost thing about which one says, 'This is it,' the case of both parties shall come before the judges; he whom the judges condemn shall pay double to his neighbor." — *Exodus 22:9*

One of the building blocks of any community is trust. Without it, relationships fall into an endless cycle of suspicion and, ultimately, ruin. The Lord provided a number of laws related to private property, the stealing of which undermines the confidence of the community in its members (Exodus 22:1–15). In these laws, God provided a mechanism to correct the wrong and make the situation right — through repayment to the offended, punishment of the offender, or both. Going through this process kept the underlying trust of the community stable. It allowed people to live their lives with confidence, rather than in fear and doubt of others. We too have a responsibility to build trust in our homes and communities. This means not only do we avoid theft and misuse of that which belongs to others, but we also seek to heal brokenness and make things right in a world permeated by wrong.

Exodus 23

"You shall sow your land for six years and gather in its yield, but on the seventh year you shall let it rest and lie fallow, so that the needy of your people may eat; and whatever they leave the beast of the field may eat. You are to do the same with your vineyard and your olive grove." — *Exodus 23:10–11*

A relationship with God concerns a great deal more than how much time we spend praying or reading our Bibles. Believers are people who commit their lives to God — not just in overtly spiritual pursuits, but also in the mundane tasks of life. For the ancient Hebrews, following God included their manner of working the land. Every seventh year, God's people were to let the land rest. This had multiple benefits. It forced the people to trust God to provide for the sabbatical year. But it also offered poor people and wild animals an opportunity to sustain themselves through the land. For this group, every seventh year was a blessing. Often greed, habit, and uncertainty leave us so focused on ourselves that we don't make allowance for those less fortunate. Take the time to seek out opportunities to help the needy in your community. With sacrifice, trust grows.

Exodus 24

Then [Moses] took the book of the covenant and read it in the hearing of the people; and they said, "All that the LORD has spoken we will do, and we will be obedient!" —*Exodus 24:7*

A relationship with God implies obedience. This was true in the garden of Eden (Genesis 2:16–17), remained a constant with Abraham (17:1), and is reaffirmed by the people of Israel in this chapter of Exodus. God has always taken the initiative in pursuing a relationship with humanity. Once God establishes the relationship, He expects His people to live in a way consistent with how He created them. When the Hebrews stopped at Sinai, God presented them with an opportunity to enter into a covenant relationship with Him. He laid out the conditions, and the people responded with an enthusiastic assurance of their own obedience. And while they failed in their commitment, their initial response was correct. As we consider our relationships with God today, we should share the aspiration of the Hebrews at Sinai—a desire to love and honor God with all our hearts, souls, and strength.

Exodus 25

"Three cups shall be shaped like almond blossoms in the one branch, a bulb and a flower, and three cups shaped like almond blossoms in the other branch, a bulb and a flower — so for six branches going out from the lampstand." —Exodus 25:33

God's instructions to build the tabernacle seem especially distant to us — the ark of the covenant has long been lost, while God's instructions for making tables, veils, and bowls find little traction for today's Christian. However, even directions for building a lampstand to light the inside of the tabernacle have much to offer us. The Lord commanded the people to construct the lampstand in decorative fashion, using the shape of an almond blossom as inspiration for the design of the light fixture. When God conceived of the place His people would worship, He made sure to include adornments and other elements that would beautify the space. By making a worship space — or any space — attractive, God's people "remake" those spaces, bringing a freshness that was previously lacking. God is in the process of remaking His people, and our commitment to beautifying all spaces — worship and otherwise — falls in line with His redemptive work in the world.

Exodus 26

"You shall hang up the veil under the clasps, and shall bring in the ark of the testimony there within the veil; and the veil shall serve for you as a partition between the holy place and the holy of holies." —Exodus 26:33

When God gave the plans for the tabernacle, He directed the people to make a veil that would separate the Holy Place — the main temple room—from the Holy of Holies, or the Holiest Place—the smaller room that housed the ark of the covenant. Solomon continued this design in the Jerusalem temple (2 Chronicles 3:14), and it was retained in the temple of Jesus's day. This veil cordoned off the place where the people could encounter God, leaving Him inaccessible to all but the high priest. However, when Jesus died, the gospel narratives tell us that the temple veil was torn in two, representing the worldwide access to God that people everywhere could have through Christ (Matthew 27:51; Mark 15:38; Luke 23:45). As believers in Christ, we can approach the Holy One in prayer from wherever we might be, knowing that Jesus's death and resurrection allow us to approach God with confidence (Hebrews 4:14–16).

Exodus 27

"You shall charge the sons of Israel, that they bring you clear oil of beaten olives for the light, to make a lamp burn continually. In the tent of meeting, outside the veil which is before the testimony . . . it shall be a perpetual statute throughout their generations for the sons of Israel." —Exodus 27:20–21

When the Hebrews built the tabernacle—and eventually the temple—the enclosed structure needed light. So God directed them to build a lamp and keep it lit perpetually. The priests were to ensure the lamp had adequate fuel. This practice maintained the worship space by providing necessary light. Moreover, the maintenance of the lighting was itself an act of worship. The Hebrew people were to pass down the proper and continual worship of God through the generations. In other words, just like believers today, the Hebrews had a responsibility to pass on the practice of faith to their children. As parents and church members, we must perpetually fan the flame of faith in the lives of children by teaching them *how* we worship — through the preaching of the Word, the proclamation of the gospel, the expression of creed and song, and the regular practice of baptism and the Lord's Supper.

Exodus 28

"You shall make holy garments for Aaron your brother, for glory and for beauty." — *Exodus 28:2*

God chose Aaron and his sons to serve as priests in the tabernacle (Exodus 28:1), and the Lord concerned Himself with the priests' outward appearance as they ministered in front of the people. He wanted to ensure that their clothes demonstrated glory and beauty, as well as consecrated them, setting them apart for the service of God (28:3). In Old Testament worship, adornments were intended to draw the attention of worshipers beyond themselves to the glorious beauty of God. Through captivating objects of physical beauty, people would be drawn to the truths displayed in the actions and words of the priests. Today, we often give little thought to the presence of physical beauty in worship, preferring instead to focus only on immaterial aspects, such as sermons and songs. Cultivating an appreciation of beauty in our worship can draw us to God through that which is uncommon and different from everyday life.

Exodus 29

"Then you shall take some of the blood that is on the altar and some of the anointing oil, and sprinkle it on Aaron and on his garments and on his sons and on his sons' garments with him; so he and his garments shall be consecrated, as well as his sons and his sons' garments with him." —*Exodus 29:21*

In both Judaism and Christianity, sacrifice has long been associated with setting a person or a people apart. When the Lord directed Moses to anoint the newly elected priests with blood and oil, it was for the purpose of consecrating—or setting apart—those priests for special service to God. Similarly, followers of Christ have been set apart by Christ's work on the cross. He sacrificed Himself for us, shedding His blood on our behalf, and that fact should lead to our being a people set apart for His service. To be a set-apart people, we need not be pastoral officials or worship leaders like those in Exodus 29. Believers should live sanctified lives, no matter our circumstances or roles in the church, separating ourselves from evil practices and thoughts and devoting ourselves to righteous living (2 Corinthians 6:16–7:1). In this kind of living, Christ's sacrifice shines all the brighter.

Exodus 30

"When you take a census of the sons of Israel to number them, then each one of them shall give a ransom for himself to the LORD. . . . You shall take the atonement money from the sons of Israel and shall give it for the service of the tent of meeting, that it may be a memorial." —*Exodus 30:12, 16*

Our deeds matter. They matter today, and they mattered in the Old Testament era. The census offering in this section of Exodus served as an "atonement" or substitute — not a substitute that saved from sin, but one that illustrated the working of God's grace in the lives of His people. Those who were counted were compelled to participate in the offering, giving to God what He required. The question for God's people, when faced with any of God's requirements, is the same today as it was then: *Will we fulfill His desire with our whole hearts?* As believers in Christ, we follow God with our hearts and our actions. Some Christians fall to the temptation of searching for the least common denominator; they have a "what-do-I-need-to-do-to-be-saved" perspective. This minimum-standard approach distorts God's intentions for His people and creates a church not fully committed to Christ. Let's pursue the higher, more difficult path by whole-heartedly fulfilling God's requirements.

Exodus 31

"I have filled [Bezalel] with the Spirit of God in wisdom, in understanding, in knowledge, and in all kinds of craftsmanship, to make artistic designs. . . . And in the hearts of all who are skillful I have put skill, that they may make all that I have commanded you."

— *Exodus 31:3 – 4, 6*

God's instructions for building the temple included numerous jobs that had to be done in order to complete the project. Some tasks required skilled artisans, people willing to use their giftedness in various arts and crafts to produce materials for adorning the tabernacle. Even from the earliest days of the Hebrews, the arts were central to life and worship — a value that came directly from the instruction of God. These artisans manipulated physical elements like stone, wood, and metal to create objects of beauty. In turn, those objects continually served as a testimony to the beauty of God, uplifting the people who saw them and worshiped in their presence. God's acknowledgement of Bezalel should remind believers both to produce and appreciate beautiful works of artistry and skill. Such pursuits enhance our worship and strengthen the testimony of God in our disordered world.

Exodus 32

"I said to them, 'Whoever has any gold, let them tear it off.' So they gave it to me, and I threw it into the fire, and out came this calf."
— *Exodus 32:24*

Human beings have always rationalized sin (Genesis 3:12), and Aaron's creation of the golden calf presents one of the clearest examples of rationalization in all of Scripture. With Moses away communing with God, the people of Israel asked Aaron to fashion an idol for them to worship. Without hesitation, Aaron told the people to gather their gold earrings; he then used a graving tool to make the golden calf from what they collected (Exodus 32:1–4). When Moses returned to see the people worshiping this object, he confronted his brother. Aaron claimed that the calf jumped from the fire by itself, a response which revealed his desire to lessen his own culpability. Aaron's rationalization didn't change the reality — or the consequences — of his sin. Three thousand of his people died that day as a result of their idolatry. Rationalization merely delays our final reckoning with the reality of our need for God's redeeming grace.

Exodus 33

Then Moses said to the LORD . . . "Now therefore, I pray You, if I have found favor in Your sight, let me know Your ways that I may know You. . . . Consider too, that this nation is Your people. . . For how then can it be known that I have found favor in Your sight, I and Your people? Is it not by Your going with us?"

—Exodus 33:12–13, 16

Calling out the obstinacy of the people, God commanded them to continue the journey without Him. They deserved God's judgment, but Moses showed his devotion. Moses did three key things in his prayer: he trusted in God's previous word to him, he interceded for his people, and he asked God to accompany the people on their journey to the promised land. Moses understood that the welfare of his people depended not on his own leadership, but completely on God's going with them. In Moses's work for God's people, he wanted to ensure he was faithfully following God every step of the way. Moses's willingness to humble himself by taking this stance reveals his love for God and God's people; Moses considered others better than himself. True devotion to God comes through such humility. We, too, must seek out the best, not first for ourselves, but for others.

Exodus 34

"Watch yourself that you make no covenant with the inhabitants of the land into which you are going, or it will become a snare in your midst."

—Exodus 34:12

As they moved toward the promised land, the people of Israel faced a difficult situation. They were to enter a land filled with people who did not share in their worship or their ideals.

The Canaanites were a people who had little value for human life—engaging in dehumanizing practices like human sacrifice and temple prostitution. So God told the people to be ready to guard themselves, giving them instructions on how to have a future in the land—without the ways of the Canaanites (Exodus 34:11–17). However, when the people of Israel entered the land, they compromised their faithfulness to God by placing themselves under obligation to certain people among the Canaanites. We, too, live in a world filled with people who care little for the things of God. Christians must honor God in our relationships, watching out so that our connections with nonbelievers do not become snares but rather opportunities for them to see the light of the gospel.

Exodus 35

The Israelites, all the men and women, whose heart moved them to bring material for all the work, which the Lord had commanded through Moses to be done, brought a freewill offering to the Lord.
—*Exodus 35:29*

When God commanded the people to build the tabernacle, they were in the middle of the Sinai Desert. Resources were scarce. If they were to accomplish the task, they would have to give from their own stores, which had been blessed when they left Egypt (Exodus 12:35–36). It was an opportunity for generosity. Their remote location could easily have tempted them to horde their possessions and look out for their own interests above those of their community. Such a lean experience might even have caused them to ignore the clear direction of God. In this instance, though, the people were humble and willing to give from the heart. And they gave so much that Moses had to tell them to stop (Exodus 36:6). In the same way, we can look for opportunities to give generously in God's honor, even if we find ourselves in a desert-like time of limited resources.

Exodus 36

So Moses issued a command, and a proclamation was circulated throughout the camp, saying, "Let no man or woman any longer perform work for the contributions of the sanctuary." Thus the people were restrained from bringing any more. — Exodus 36:6

In our modern world, many people operate on the principle that we should acquire as much as we can get. However, the biblical picture of God's people illustrates another set of values. Rather than seeking to consume every resource at our disposal, God's people should operate based on need. The apostle Paul made clear the importance of contentment for the believer (Philippians 4:12), and this story about the building of the tabernacle illustrates a similar point. When Moses called for more materials, the people responded with extreme generosity. But rather than continue to accept gifts beyond the needs for the tabernacle, Moses actually commanded the people to stop giving when the builders had gathered enough. When was the last time a religious organization happened upon a time of prosperity and directed people to take their gifts elsewhere? Such a radical approach to our resources would likely revolutionize the church and people's perception of it.

Exodus 37

Now Bezalel made the ark of acacia wood; its length was two and a half cubits, and its width one and a half cubits, and its height one and a half cubits; and he overlaid it with pure gold inside and out, and made a gold molding for it all around. —Exodus 37:1–2

Worship stood at the center of Israelite life. The construction of the worship space—the tabernacle and its implements—illustrates the central importance of God to this community. God's people did not simply throw together the tabernacle with whatever they could easily or quickly find. God directed them toward the best materials. And the ark of the covenant, the place where God's glory would dwell, was no exception. They made the ark out of acacia—a very durable wood—and then overlaid it with gold inside and out before adding other elements, which were also made of gold (Exodus 37:6–9). How do you and your church illustrate that God is central to the life of your community? Just as the Israelites created a worship space of great value, we too can pour value into our worship spaces as a physical representation of our desire to give God glory and draw others to Him.

Exodus 38

He cast four rings on the four ends of the bronze grating as holders for the poles. He made the poles of acacia wood and overlaid them with bronze. He inserted the poles into the rings on the sides of the altar, with which to carry it. —Exodus 38:5–7

When the Israelites received the command to build the tabernacle, the new building had to be portable. God had no intention for His people to settle down in the Sinai desert. So God directed the people to create ways to transport the structure and its pieces. God wanted the people to have a shared worship space, a place to humble themselves as a community and acknowledge Him as God. God's people today also need places to worship together. We are no longer limited to a temple among one nation's people. And yet, so often, people who call themselves Christians avoid places of worship — churches — for any number of reasons. If it was important enough for the Israelites to have a place of worship in the desert, it is important enough for Christians today to find a place where they can worship God among His people.

Exodus 39

And Moses examined all the work and behold, they had done it; just as the LORD had commanded, this they had done. So Moses blessed them.   *—Exodus 39:43*

The construction of the tabernacle was the most significant and complex building project in the history of the Israelites up to that point. And yet, despite the enormity of the project and the remoteness of their location, the people worked with extreme care and built it exactly to the specifications God provided. Too often we make too little of the Lord's commands. We treat them flippantly. We apply them to our lives lightly. We don't think seriously about how they should work themselves out in our lives. Such a shallow rendering of God's Word in our everyday lives leaves us wanting when we truly consider the kind of people God wants us to be. May we each take it upon ourselves to carefully consider God's commands to His people, that we might follow them from the deepest recesses of our hearts to the slightest movements of our hands and feet.

Exodus 40

Then the cloud covered the tent of meeting, and the glory of the LORD
filled the tabernacle. Moses was not able to enter the tent of meeting
because the cloud had settled on it, and the glory of the LORD filled
the tabernacle. — *Exodus 40:34–35*

People — believers and otherwise — often think of the God in the
Old Testament as a distant figure, unconcerned with the plight or
direction of humanity. Such a perspective is both unbiblical and
unchristian. God came near to His people numerous times before
Israel built the tabernacle (Genesis 3:8; 18:1; Exodus 19:18).
The Lord also descended here in Exodus 40, once His people
completed the tabernacle. In these key moments and many others, God is always present. What was true then is true today.
As Christians, we believe the Lord also descended in the most
magnificent way possible — through the person of Jesus Christ
(John 1:14). He has come near to us, so we are able to draw
near to Him. Wherever we go, whatever we do, we can know the
closeness of God's presence and His intimate care for His people.
May that give us confidence as we live for Him and serve others.

Leviticus

Leviticus 1

" 'If his offering is a burnt offering from the herd, he shall offer it, a male without defect . . . that he may be accepted before the LORD.' "
—*Leviticus 1:3*

How could an Israelite know if God had accepted him or her? The burnt offering made it clear. The various animals used as sacrifices in the burnt offering provided for the different financial levels of the people. No one was barred from coming to God because of income or status; yet *no one* could approach Him without a sacrifice. Scripture repeatedly stresses that the burnt offering consumed by the fire became a "soothing aroma to the Lord" (Leviticus 1:9, 13, 17). In other words, God was pleased to accept anyone who came to Him through His prescribed sacrifice. The same is true today. The sacrifices of Leviticus had their ultimate fulfillment in Jesus Christ, who sacrificed His life on the cross. The resurrection proves that God accepted Christ's sacrifice; therefore, we can know—and never wonder—that God accepts all who trust in Christ for forgiveness of sins (Romans 4:25 – 5:1).

Leviticus 2

" 'He shall . . . take from it his handful of its fine flour and of its oil with all of its frankincense. And the priest shall offer it up in smoke as its memorial portion on the altar, an offering by fire of a soothing aroma to the Lord.' "
—*Leviticus 2:2*

Someone accepted by God through the burnt offering could respond to God's grace through a grain offering. Often coming from the first gleanings of harvest, the fine flour and oil signified the very best the worshiper had to offer (Leviticus 2:14). The Lord expected the Hebrews to offer their very best as an expression of their dedication and gratitude. As Christians, we also respond to the mercies of God by offering "a living and holy sacrifice"—that is, our bodies (Romans 12:1). By living our lives in obedience to God, we give Him the very best we have to offer. Even our financial gifts serve as "a fragrant aroma, an acceptable sacrifice, well-pleasing to God" (Philippians 4:18). God is pleased when believers are so grateful to Him for His mercies that they offer Him their lives—the best they have—as an expression of gratitude and dedication.

Leviticus 3

" 'Now if his offering is a sacrifice of peace offerings . . . then Aaron's sons shall offer it up in smoke on the altar on the burnt offering . . . a soothing aroma to the Lord.' "   —*Leviticus 3:1, 5*

The optional peace offering allowed the worshiper to celebrate fellowship with God. Placed atop the burnt offering, the peace offering pictured a timeless principle: peace with God comes at the price of shed blood (Hebrews 9:22). While this "thanksgiving peace" offering cooked (Leviticus 7:15), the worshiper audibly gave thanks for what God had done. The offering was then enjoyed as a communal meal, which came with a warning that, if ignored, could result in premature death (Leviticus 7:19–21). Believers today enjoy peace with God through the death of our final sacrifice, Jesus (Romans 5:1). We celebrate that peace through a communal meal—the Lord's Supper or Communion—in which we consume elements representing the body and blood of our Lord (1 Corinthians 11:23–25). Unlike the peace offering, the Lord's Supper is mandatory—but it does carry a warning of premature death if ignored (11:27–32).

Leviticus 4

"'If a person sins unintentionally in any of the things which the LORD has commanded not to be done . . . then let him offer to the LORD a bull without defect as a sin offering for the sin he has committed.'"
—*Leviticus 4:2–3*

We often associate guilt only with the will. But God holds people responsible for unintentional sins as well. Better rendered the "purification offering," the sin offering dealt with two issues: forgiveness from unintentional sins and cleansing from ceremonial uncleanness. An "unclean" status did not necessarily relate to sin. For example, giving birth, having a skin disease, or burying a dead relative all rendered a person "unclean." However, the "non-normalness" of such conditions required the cleansing of the purification offering. An unintentional sin required the sacrifice plus a confession once the sinner became aware of that sin (Leviticus 5:5). As Christians, we have confidence that our unintentional sins and physical impurities needn't exclude us from fellowship with God. Because of Jesus's sacrifice on our behalf, all we need to do to experience restoration in our fellowship with God is confess our known sins to Him. He promises to forgive us and cleanse us "from all unrighteousness"—including those sins we don't know to confess (Hebrews 10:22; 1 John 1:9).

Leviticus 5

"He shall make restitution . . . and shall add to it a fifth part of it and give it to the priest. The priest shall then make atonement for him with the ram of the guilt offering, and it will be forgiven him."

—*Leviticus 5:16*

The guilt offering provided forgiveness for the individual who unintentionally defrauded God and later came to realize it—as well as for the outright cheat who robbed a fellow citizen (Leviticus 6:1–7). The guilt offering caused the individual to look beyond the sin to the damage it caused. The sinner not only sought forgiveness; he or she *first* paid full restitution, plus an additional percentage. Even today, restitution remains a biblical priority *before* coming to worship (Matthew 5:23–24 applies by principle). Although the Messiah's death served as our final guilt offering (Isaiah 53:10), God's forgiveness doesn't negate our obligation to repay our debts. Reparation remains our responsibility and also serves as evidence of true repentance (Luke 19:8–9). If we look at our past and see financial compromise, paying back what we've taken—either from God or from people—is a matter of obedience and integrity.

Leviticus 6

" 'The fire on the altar shall be kept burning on it. It shall not go out, but the priest shall burn wood on it every morning; and he shall lay out the burnt offering on it. . . . Fire shall be kept burning continually on the altar; it is not to go out.' "   —*Leviticus 6:12–13*

Although priests had many duties, keeping the brazen altar's fire burning—providing constant access to God through sacrifice—remained central to their job. In the same way, believers today must keep the message of the cross central to our service. As a "holy" and "royal priesthood" (1 Peter 2:5, 9), Christians should stay ready to assist those seeking access to God (3:15–16). Of course, we can do social work, help with physical needs, and volunteer at soup kitchens, but *the central focus* of our activities and ministries must be Christ (1 Corinthians 1:17–19; Galatians 6:14). Without the cross—and its message of salvation—the church offers nothing more than temporary relief to a world bound for hell. Access to God through the sacrifice of Christ must remain an ever-ready message on our lips. We should never let that fire go out.

Leviticus 7

" 'You shall not eat any fat from an ox, a sheep or a goat. . . . You are not to eat any blood, either of bird or animal, in any of your dwellings.' " —Leviticus 7:23, 26

Commands not to eat the fat or blood of animals had nothing to do with health or dietary concerns. A fat animal represented one that was well fed—the best of the flock. God deserved the best, and eating the fat represented eating what was God's. The command not to eat blood recognized the sanctity of life, for blood represented life (Deuteronomy 12:23). Life remains God's alone to give and to take. Because every sacrifice represented the worshiper who offered it, giving God the fat and the blood meant giving God the very best and one's own life. Not giving God the best sacrifices resulted in rebuke (Malachi 1:8). Even today, we are to give God the best of our lives—including our time, our treasure, and our talents (1 Corinthians 12:7; 2 Corinthians 8:7; Ephesians 5:15–16).

Leviticus 8

Moses slaughtered it and took some of its blood and put it on the lobe
of Aaron's right ear, and on the thumb of his right hand and on the
big toe of his right foot.   *—Leviticus 8:23*

In the ordination service of the priests, applying blood to parts
of the body represented a specific dedication to God. Blood on
the right ear showed that people devoted to God are open to
hearing Him. By principle, believers today should always listen
with the intent to obey (Psalm 78:1–2; James 1:22–25). Blood
on the right thumb demonstrated that people devoted to God
employ their hands for His work. The thumb is essential to any
manual labor—and still today, all a believer's work is to be done
for God (1 Peter 4:10–11). Blood on the priest's right big toe
indicated that people devoted to God use their feet to follow
Him. The dedication of our bodies to God is something He takes
seriously. As the sacrificial blood smeared on the bodies of the
priests demonstrated, *all* of who we are belongs to God's service
(1 Corinthians 6:20).

Leviticus 9

Then Aaron lifted up his hands toward the people and blessed
them. . . . Then fire came out from before the LORD and consumed the
burnt offering and the portions of fat on the altar; and when all
the people saw it, they shouted [for joy] and fell on their faces.
                                          —Leviticus 9:22, 24

Aaron's blessing on the people in this chapter likely included
what God later commanded—a blessing of God's grace and
peace upon them (Numbers 6:22–26). When God appeared

before the people and fire consumed the sacrifice, they understood that Aaron's blessing of grace and peace came only through the forgiveness the sacrifice had made possible. The people responded by shouting for joy and falling before God in worship. Many of the apostle Paul's epistles begin with a greeting of "grace and peace" from God and Jesus Christ—reminiscent of the priestly blessing rooted in God's sacrifice (Galatians 1:3; Ephesians 1:2). The grace and peace we receive from God—and the worship we return to Him—stem from the sacrifice of Christ on the cross. God's blessing of forgiveness comes out of His love and mercy (John 3:16). The worship we offer God comes out of our gratitude for His grace (Hebrews 12:28).

Leviticus 10

Now Nadab and Abihu, the sons of Aaron . . . offered strange fire before the LORD, which He had not commanded them. And fire came out from the presence of the LORD and consumed them, and they died before the LORD.   *— Leviticus 10:1–2*

The "strange fire" Aaron's sons offered was unapproved fire that came from somewhere other than the brazen altar. The only fire allowed in the tabernacle was the fire God had ignited in Leviticus 9:24. Nadab and Abihu knew how to approach God, but they ignored what they knew—likely because inebriation had impaired their judgment (Leviticus 10:9–10). God's capital sentence may appear harsh, but the passage reveals that God takes His Word seriously. What proved true in the garden of Eden played out in this account, and it lingers in our lives today.

Convenient alternatives to the hard work of obedience eventually reveal themselves as the destroyers of our lives. The deaths of Aaron's sons taught a valuable lesson to the priests and Israelites of Leviticus that is still true for us today: God expects us to treat Him as holy by obeying His Word and honoring Him in front of others (Leviticus 10:3).

Leviticus 11

"'You shall not make yourselves unclean with any of the swarming things that swarm on the earth. For I am the LORD who brought you up from the land of Egypt to be your God; thus you shall be holy, for I am holy.'" —*Leviticus 11:44–45*

Kosher laws may strike Christians today as strange, but these laws served a vital, practical purpose. Put simply, we spend more time with those who share our tastes. And the more time we spend with a specific group, the greater their influence on us. If the Israelites didn't like the foods of nearby godless cultures, they would be more likely to avoid them and escape their influence. Acquired tastes protected God's people. Even though Jesus later put bacon back on the menu, He understood kosher foods illustrated the higher principle of holy living (Mark 7:18–23). We're still called to imitate God's holiness in all aspects of life—even eating (1 Corinthians 10:31; 1 Timothy 4:4). In Leviticus 11, Moses pointed to the deliverance from Egypt as motivation for obedience. Peter quoted this passage, comparing the Passover lamb to Jesus's death for us, reminding us that our redemption should motivate us to holy living (1 Peter 1:14–19).

Leviticus 12

"'She shall be cleansed from the flow of her blood. This is the law for her who bears a child, whether a male or a female. But if she cannot afford a lamb, then she shall take two turtledoves or two young pigeons . . . and she will be clean.'" —*Leviticus 12:7–8*

Because only sacrificial blood was allowed in God's presence, blood loss during and after childbirth prevented a mother from entering the tabernacle. Moreover, healing from delivery is not a woman's usual condition, and all who entered the tabernacle had to be cleansed of "non-normalness." So after a number of days, a new mother could bring an offering for her ritual cleansing and resume normal worship. God provided a way for any mother—rich or poor—to be made whole again and enter His presence. Mary offered such a sacrifice after she gave birth to Jesus (Luke 2:21–24). Leviticus 12 reveals that God's purpose for His followers includes being made whole physically—not just spiritually. He has made provision for His people to dwell in resurrected bodies when He brings about the New Heaven and the New Earth (Daniel 12:13; 1 Corinthians 15:50–53; Philippians 3:20–21; Revelation 21:1–5).

Leviticus 13

"The priest shall look at the mark on the skin of the body, and if . . . it is an infection of leprosy; when the priest has looked at him, he shall pronounce him unclean." —*Leviticus 13:3*

Because diseases entered the world as a result of sin, they are symptoms of human alienation and separation from God—which is death. For this reason, a diseased Israelite stayed outside the camp and remained untouchable, much like a corpse, until he or she was clean. Holiness in Israel was symbolized by being whole—or "normal," as God defined it. Only flawless animals were sacrificed; only physically normal priests could serve; only people in normal conditions could worship; only normal clothing could be worn; and only normal houses could be inhabited. If any of these essentials were not normal—or were "unclean"—the situation required action. By principle, nothing has changed. Because God is holy, we must be like Him to be with Him (Matthew 5:48). But how? Through Jesus's death and resurrection, God made a way for us to become clean and meet His standard (Titus 3:5).

Leviticus 14

"[The priest] shall dip them and the live bird in the blood of the bird that was slain. . . . He shall then sprinkle seven times the one who is to be cleansed from the leprosy and shall pronounce him clean, and shall let the live bird go free over the open field."

—*Leviticus 14:6–7*

In this ritual, the two birds together represented the sick person and revealed that life is in God's hands. One bird's death signified what would happen apart from God's gracious intervention. The other bird's freedom symbolized healing from disease and a new life with God. The opportunity is timeless. When Christ healed people during His ministry on earth, He gave a preview of what He will do for all who will enter His kingdom. Those who were unclean He cleansed, and those who were sick He healed. Just as Christ's resurrection offered a preview of all resurrections, so every healing and every physical recovery serves as a foretaste of what God will do on a cosmic scale for all believers before we enter heaven. We will be set free like a bird from all of our physical diseases and distresses—welcome to enter God's presence forever.

Leviticus 15

This is the law for the one with a discharge, and for the man who has a seminal emission . . . and for the woman who is ill because of menstrual impurity, and for the one who has a discharge, whether a male or a female, or a man who lies with an unclean woman.

—*Leviticus 15:32–33*

The personal nature of this chapter shows that certain bodily discharges—though natural—rendered a person ceremonially unclean and unable to fellowship with God apart from purification. The text makes no judgments, except to indicate that these discharges suspended intimate relations in marriage, as well as communion with God in the tabernacle. The command to suspend sexual intercourse during the wife's monthly cycle indicates the timeless truth that, even in the marriage relationship where sex is blessed, self-control is required (Leviticus 18:19; 20:18). Our culture has elevated sex to a right by defining it as a "need," thereby falsely justifying immoral gratification if morality fails to satisfy. But biblically, true needs are those without which we would die—either physically or spiritually. Scripture presents sex not as a need, but as a legitimate, godly desire that can and must be controlled (Proverbs 5:15–19; 1 Thessalonians 4:3–5).

Leviticus 16

"For it is on this day that atonement shall be made for you to cleanse you; you will be clean from all your sins before the LORD*. It is to be a sabbath of solemn rest for you, that you may humble your souls."*
—Leviticus 16:30–31

The holiest day in the Hebrew calendar was the annual Day of Atonement called *Yom Kippur*. On this holy day, the only required fast for God's people, the Israelites humbled themselves in preparation for God's provision of complete forgiveness. The blood of one goat cleansed the tabernacle from the impurities of dwelling among a sinful people. The other live goat, called the "scapegoat," would bear the sins of the people as a man led it away into the wilderness. These rituals made the impossible possible — God forgave sins completely. The ultimate Day of Atonement was fulfilled through the death and resurrection of Jesus, and forgiveness is possible by faith in Him (Romans 3:21–26). Because of Jesus's once-for-all "sacrifice of atonement" (3:25 NIV), every believer has the assurance of forgiveness from sins and the freedom to serve the living God (Hebrews 9:11–14).

Leviticus 17

" 'The life of the flesh is in the blood, and I have given it to you on the altar to make atonement for your souls.' . . . Therefore I said to the sons of Israel, 'No person among you may eat blood.' "
—Leviticus 17:11–12

Life belongs to God alone, and the command to abstain from eating blood reflected this truth. Life is in the blood, so in Leviticus, a loss of blood represented a loss of life. Furthermore, sacrificial blood had to be recognized and respected as such — or premature death could follow. Although believers today are not prohibited from eating rare steaks, the principles of the source of life and the sanctity of sacrificial blood are timeless. Jesus told His followers to "drink" His blood — a simple metaphor that represented a person's acceptance of Jesus's sacrificial death. All believers are required to participate in Communion (or the Lord's Supper) and drink the cup that represents Christ's blood shed on our behalf. To partake without a personal examination is to participate in a manner unworthy of Christ's sacrificial blood. Without repentance of this sin, God may prematurely take the life of a believer (1 Corinthians 11:23 – 32).

Leviticus 18

"'You shall not have intercourse with your neighbor's wife, to be defiled with her. . . . I am the LORD. You shall not lie with a male as one lies with a female; it is an abomination. Also you shall not have intercourse with any animal.'" — *Leviticus 18:20 – 23*

When Leviticus shifts from public worship to private holiness, the subject matter gets intensely personal. The commands for sexual purity represented more than good advice to the Hebrews. These commands were a matter of loyalty to the God who had redeemed His people. In this chapter's blunt list of prohibitions, we quickly see little difference between the immoralities of then and now. Any sexual expression outside the context of a monogamous marriage sidesteps God's intentions and His commands and, therefore, is sin. Although the Lord grants forgiveness through Christ for any of these perversions (1 Corinthians 6:9 – 11), it's helpful to remember that the commands in Leviticus were written to a people already redeemed. In the same way, the New Testament repeatedly urges Christians to live lives of absolute sexual purity (Matthew 5:28; 1 Corinthians 6:18–20; 1 Thessalonians 4:1–8; 2 Timothy 2:22). One of the greatest ways we reveal our loyalty to God is through our sexuality.

Leviticus 19

"Speak to all the congregation of the sons of Israel and say to them, 'You shall be holy, for I the Lord *your God am holy.'"*

—*Leviticus 19:2*

Throughout Leviticus 19, the Lord recaps the Ten Commandments, giving illustrations and reiterating (sixteen times) the motivation for obedience: "I am the Lord your God." Moreover, the Hebrews learned the standard that undergirds all morality—God's holiness. Whether the laws required spending less than one earns, helping believers in need, telling the truth, paying the bills, refraining from vengeance, or loving one's neighbor, each instruction revealed something about God's character or God's will. Many Old Testament directives are echoed in the New Testament. In fact, nine of the Ten Commandments are repeated. Timeless truths lie beneath every Old Testament command and remain applicable today, though the specific command may no longer apply. We obey God not simply because He says so—though that would be enough—but because we understand that every commandment reflects God's holy character (1 Peter 1:14–16).

Leviticus 20

"'As for the person who turns to mediums and to spiritists, to play the harlot after them, I will also set My face against that person. . . . You shall consecrate yourselves therefore and be holy, for I am the LORD *your God.'"* — *Leviticus 20:6 – 7*

The mention of mediums and spiritists at both the beginning and end of this chapter indicates that the primary concern of this section stems from pagan beliefs that opened the door to violations of God's laws. Between these bookend commands, Moses sketched various decadences that violate God's holiness. This arrangement of verses reveals a cause-and-effect relationship between how God's people think and how they act. The command in verse 7 to "consecrate yourselves therefore" meant that the Hebrew people were to separate themselves from the pagan sources of supernatural information, because the Lord was their God — their sole source of truth. What was true then is true now — wrong beliefs always lead to wrong behavior. What we choose to think on will shape our beliefs and will inescapably direct our actions (Romans 12:1–2; Philippians 4:8). We can shun worldly practices only by saturating our minds with truth from God.

Leviticus 21

"'No [priest] shall defile himself for a dead person. . . . He shall take a wife in her virginity. A widow, or a divorced woman, or one who is profaned by harlotry, these he may not take; but rather he is to marry a virgin of his own people.'" — *Leviticus 21:1, 13 – 14*

The stipulations of marrying a virgin and not burying a relative were particular to a priest, but they had nothing to do with his responsibilities in the tabernacle. Rather, these laws reflected his personal life. This shows that the priesthood represented more than an occupation; it was a way of life. God sees Christians as a holy priesthood, and as such, no division exists between our spiritual and secular lives (1 Peter 2:5, 9). Every part of our lives is to be dedicated to God—including how we treat death, whom we marry, and where we work. As representatives of God, we carry our spiritual lives with us to our homes, our workplaces, the movies, the market, our churches—*everywhere* we go. Like the priests of old, the spiritual and the secular cannot be divided in the life of a believer. We are Christians everywhere.

Leviticus 22

"Tell Aaron and his sons to be careful with the holy gifts of the sons of Israel, which they dedicate to Me, so as not to profane My holy name; I am the LORD.... 'No layman, however, is to eat the holy gift.'" —Leviticus 22:2, 10

This chapter describes gifts offered to God. Each offering had to be a flawless animal, representing that God deserved the best, not the leftovers. Moreover, no one was to treat the sacrifices as a common meal. They were holy. Only the priests—not laymen—ate these sacrifices, and even then, only priests who were ceremonially clean could eat. Similarly, in the present age, only the royal priesthood of believers—the body of Christ—should participate in the rituals Christ has ordained for us. Jesus gave Christians two rituals, both of which have prerequisites. The first, baptism, occurs once and requires a person to believe in Jesus Christ. The second, the Lord's Supper, occurs repeatedly and requires a Christian to be in fellowship with Christ — compelling personal reflection prior to participation (1 Corinthians 11:27–28).

Leviticus 23

"'In the first month, on the fourteenth day of the month at twilight is the LORD's Passover. Then on the fifteenth day of the same month there is the Feast of Unleavened Bread to the LORD; for seven days you shall eat unleavened bread.'"   *— Leviticus 23:5–6*

Every year, the nation of Israel gathered and celebrated their redemption from slavery in Egypt. The Feast of Passover involved killing a lamb and eating a communal meal, remembering how God had delivered His people through the blood of the lamb. The Feast of Unleavened Bread immediately followed. Every day for one week, the Hebrews would eat bread without leaven, also called yeast. Removing the leaven, which has corrupting effects on bread, came to represent the elimination of all spiritually corrupting things from believers' lives. The apostle Paul used these feasts to illustrate our duty as Christians. Because "Christ our Passover also has been sacrificed," we who are redeemed from sin should "celebrate the feast" (1 Corinthians 5:7–8). That is, we should remove every corrupting influence from our lives. We ought to live "with the unleavened bread of sincerity and truth." And the way Paul wrote the word *celebrate* indicates a continual action. We are to live the rest of our lives *unleavened*.

Leviticus 24

"'The one who blasphemes the name of the Lord *shall surely be put to death; all the congregation shall certainly stone him. The alien as well as the native, when he blasphemes the Name, shall be put to death.'"* —*Leviticus 24:16*

By delivering such a severe penalty, God revealed that His name is holy, for a name represents the person. The "name" of God includes His nature, His teaching, and His character. We can tell who God is by His many names in Scripture. For example, Mighty God, Everlasting Father, Prince of Peace, and *El-Shaddai*, which means, "God Almighty." As believers, everything we do should be done "in the name of the Lord Jesus" (Colossians 3:17). The New Testament gives specifics as to how we can honor the name of the Lord: in belief (John 3:18), in baptism (Matthew 28:19), in prayer (Matthew 6:9; John 14:13), in service (Acts 9:27), and in suffering (Acts 5:41). Bringing honor to Jesus's name should be the motivation for all we do, because coworkers, family, friends, neighbors, and total strangers are watching us. We should speak and act as if the Lord's reputation is at stake.

Leviticus 25

"'The land, moreover, shall not be sold permanently, for the land is Mine; for you are but aliens and sojourners with Me.'" —*Leviticus 25:23*

After His people settled in Canaan, God allowed them to work the land. But every seventh year, the land was to lie fallow (Leviticus 25:4). In 586 BC, after 490 years of His people failing to observe the sabbatical year, God exiled them for the seventy special years they had not given the land (2 Chronicles 36:20–21). All this was to show that the land belonged to God, not to those who lived on it. Although the people worked the land, it was God who provided, and to prove it, He made them stop working. Faith involves trust, and trust implies risk (from our perspective). While God is never late, He is seldom early. The Father longs for us to understand that He provides *daily* bread, not careers by which we're set for life (Luke 11:3). God may keep us on the edge of our means, for there our need for Him is often more clearly seen.[1]

Leviticus 26

"'If you walk in My statutes and keep My commandments so as to carry them out, then I shall give you rains in their season, so that the land will yield its produce and the trees of the field will bear their fruit.'"
— *Leviticus 26:3–4*

God promised to bless the Israelites based on their obedience to His Word, and that blessing came in the form of rain. One of the most important geographical features of Canaan was its lack of a significant water source. Thus, God used a simple, physical resource like rain to teach a vital, spiritual truth: He alone is the true source of life. Since water remained the most important variable in the land of Canaan, God used the climate to encourage Israel to trust and obey Him. When they disobeyed, drought followed. Talk about motivation to repent! God has already blessed Christians with every spiritual blessing in Christ (Ephesians 1:3). Our ultimate physical and material prosperity is promised in heaven (Philippians 3:20–21; Revelation 21:4). But, as a loving

Father, God disciplines unrepentant Christians while on earth so we will return to Him and "share His holiness" (Hebrews 12:10; see also 12:4–9).

Leviticus 27

"Speak to the sons of Israel and say to them, 'When a man makes a difficult vow, he shall be valued according to your valuation of persons belonging to the Lord.'" —Leviticus 27:2

If a man made a difficult or special vow in which he promised himself, his family, or any of his possessions to God, God allowed that man to "redeem" that vow with an appropriate sum of money. Although this application is no longer binding, the underlying principle of paying a vow, or keeping one's word, remains in effect for both men and women who believe in Christ. Our Lord Jesus cautioned His followers against making vows hastily, urging them simply to say yes or no (Matthew 5:33–37). As Solomon noted, "When you make a vow to God, do not be late in paying it; for He takes no delight in fools. Pay what you vow! It is better that you should not vow than that you should vow and not pay" (Ecclesiastes 5:4–5). This standard of keeping a "difficult" commitment reflects the character of our God who keeps His promises.

Numbers

Numbers 1

So Moses and Aaron took these men who had been designated by name. . . . Then they registered by ancestry in their families, by their fathers' households, according to the number of names. . . . So [Moses] numbered them in the wilderness of Sinai.

—Numbers 1:17–19

The book of Numbers derives its name from two head counts—one census taken at the beginning of the book and another toward the end, as the new generation of Israelites anticipated the conquest of Canaan. Thirty-eight years of history took place between those two sets of numbers, a period when the people of God wandered from Sinai to Transjordan. Why was a census necessary in Numbers 1? God surely knew the name of every Israelite at Sinai! God was the one who named the family delegates to help Moses and to represent their tribes (Numbers 1:4–16). The census wasn't for God's benefit; it was for the people's. It gave them a recorded history, a remembrance, and perhaps even a caution. Those are still good ideas today. Every generation is able to make more sense of their lives if they know the successes and failures of previous generations. We should all heed the lessons of those who have gone before.

Numbers 2

Thus the sons of Israel did; according to all that the LORD commanded Moses, so they camped by their standards, and so they set out, every one by his family according to his father's household.

—Numbers 2:34

The census was not an end unto itself. It was a military muster and an organizational scheme. The people of Israel had come out of slavery *en masse*; now, God intended to bring order and discipline to their ranks. The numbers recorded were specifically those qualified to fight. The people had been passive participants when God brought them out of Egypt. Now, they were being shown how to array themselves as a confident army, a force to be reckoned with, and God was their captain. Their four-hundred-year season of slavery and waiting had ended; it was time to act. That balance between anticipation and action, between waiting on God and making a move, is one of the puzzles of the Christian life. Rushing forward without God's green light is foolhardy. Delaying when God says, "Do it!" is disobedient. We wait until we know, then we step out with confidence.

Numbers 3

"Take the Levites instead of all the firstborn among the sons of Israel and the cattle of the Levites. And the Levites shall be Mine; I am the LORD."   *—Numbers 3:45*

Conspicuously, the members of the tribe of Levi were not numbered in the first census the same way as the other Israelites. The Levites were not counted to fight but to serve. God had claimed them from birth as priestly servants in lieu of the firstborn of each Israelite household. Only about two years had passed since the Passover in Exodus, and the significance of God's owning the firstborn child was clear—many in the camp would have died in Egypt had it not been for God's provision of a sacrificial substitute, the Paschal Lamb. Each Levite was as precious to God as the lives of those firstborn who were saved, and each firstborn was as precious as the blood that was shed to save him. This chain of substitution extends to us today. Our service to God is tied directly to the value He places on our lives—and He valued us enough to sacrifice His only Son.

Numbers 4

According to the commandment of the LORD through Moses, they were numbered, everyone by his serving or carrying; thus these were his numbered men, just as the LORD had commanded Moses.

—Numbers 4:49

The duties of the three clans of the Levites were specific. No shift-sharing and no departmental staff transfers were allowed. The wrappers were to wrap; the carriers were to carry; the carters were to cart. Each man clearly understood not only what he *should* do but also what he *should not* do. Notice that this demarcation of duty was not based on innate ability but on God's prescription. A broad-shouldered man from another tribe couldn't just show up and say, "I'm strong; I'll carry!" How often do we give innate ability too much consideration when we assign duties? Clearly, we want people to use their gifts and talents for God's glory! But do we also take into account God's prescriptions? A man might have a way with words, but *should* he preach, given his reputation? A woman might sing like a nightingale, but *should* she lead the worship team, given her circumstances?

Numbers 5

*"'When a man or woman commits any of the sins of mankind . . .
and that person is guilty, then he shall confess his sins which he has
committed, and he shall make restitution in full for his wrong and
add to it one-fifth of it, and give it to him whom he has wronged.'"*
—Numbers 5:6–7

In the book of Numbers, God invested order and discipline into
the community of the Israelites. For order to prevail, it must be
served by justice. Justice requires that crime is *visibly* dealt with
and that the rights of victims are upheld over the rights of per-
petrators. In this very early edition of judicial law, we recognize
at least three principles that are foundational today. First, the
pursuit of the truth: if guilty, then confess. Second, the standard
of restitution: the burden is on the perpetrator to make good
on that which has been stolen, broken, or profaned. Third, the
idea of punitive damages: equal restitution is not a deterrent—it
gives the thief a chance to break even. Would-be criminals must
risk more than they hope to gain. Paul endorsed such a principle
in Ephesians 4:28, and of course, Zaccheus became the poster
child for generous restitution in Luke 19.

Numbers 6

*"'The Nazirite shall then shave his dedicated head of hair at the
doorway of the tent of meeting, and take the dedicated hair of his
head and put it on the fire which is under the sacrifice of peace
offerings.'"*
—Numbers 6:18

Anyone was allowed to take the Nazirite vow, an expression of
temporarily heightened devotion to God, perhaps similar to fast-
ing today. The term finds its roots in a Hebrew verb meaning

"to set apart" or "to abstain." The devotee demonstrated his or her sincerity by avoiding wine, corpses (even family funerals), and haircuts. To end the season of special devotion, Nazirites brought to the tabernacle costly offerings, which consisted of their long-grown manes, along with whatever else they could afford (Numbers 6:18, 21). Such dedication was also encouraged by Christ. In Luke 9:57–62, Jesus told three would-be disciples to be willing to relinquish their security if necessary, leave the dead to themselves (even family members), and not second-guess their decision. It seems extraordinary devotion to God looks a lot like ordinary Christianity; it's open to all, but it doesn't come cheap, and it can't be carried out incognito.

Numbers 7

But [Moses] did not give any to the sons of Kohath because theirs was the service of the holy objects, which they carried on the shoulder.

—*Numbers 7:9*

The twelve tribal heads brought equipment and furnishings for the new tabernacle. The tribe of Levi brought no gifts; rather, the Levites received these items to use as they served at the altar. There were still twelve tribal heads apart from the Levites, because Jacob's grandsons—Ephraim and Manasseh—had each inherited a full tribal portion (effectively doubling their father Joseph's inheritance). Every tribe was fully invested in establishing God's court on earth, bringing oxen and carts and elaborate offerings. The Levites were given everything they needed to serve God but nothing they didn't need, and Moses distributed the items among the Levites as God directed. The duties of Kohath's sons involved carrying the sacred objects on their shoulders. Had they been given carts, they would have been tempted to use them and, thereby, violate God's plan. Sometimes we are not given *every* convenient means because God has a certain way He wants us to fulfill the task He has set before us.

Numbers 8

"Take the Levites from among the sons of Israel and cleanse them. Thus you shall do to them, for their cleansing: sprinkle purifying water on them, and let them use a razor over their whole body and wash their clothes, and they will be clean." —Numbers 8:6–7

The Levites presented themselves as outwardly washed and trimmed. Additionally, Moses made a series of sacrifices on their behalf to signify their spiritual cleansing and inward suitability for their duties. Once they had been presented to the national assembly, they were consecrated (set apart for service), and Aaron presented them before the Lord as a wave offering from the people of Israel (Numbers 8:11). In this way, the Levites became living sacrifices to God. Their lives were no longer their own; they were given totally to their ministry. Paul encouraged all believers to "present your bodies a living and holy sacrifice, acceptable to God, which is your spiritual service of worship" (Romans 12:1). We are an entire kingdom of servants along the lines of the Levites. We are not Aaronic priests—Christ has superseded their ministry as intercessors—but we are servants given to God just as the Levites were given to Him.

Numbers 9

*"'But the man who is clean and is not on a journey, and yet neglects to observe the Passover, that person shall then be cut off from his people, for he did not present the offering of the L*ORD* at its appointed time. That man will bear his sin.'"* —Numbers 9:13

The Passover was mandated as the key annual observance for Israel. Grace was built into God's stipulation—those who were *unable* to celebrate the memorial could wait a month and observe a second edition of the ceremony (Numbers 9:10–11). However, such grace did not apply to those who *wouldn't.* Anyone who *could* observe the Passover but chose not to was removed from the community of faith. Willingness to partake of the Passover meal and to remember God's miraculous deliverance out of Egypt was the principal barometer of faith and involvement. The Passover was the great symbol of the work that Christ would eventually do, and the underlying terms are still in place. God extends grace; He offers second chances. But those who can believe yet refuse to *will bear their own sin.*

Numbers 10

*Then Moses said to Hobab the son of Reuel the Midianite, Moses' father-in-law, "We are setting out to the place of which the L*ORD* said, 'I will give it to you.' . . . Please do not leave us, inasmuch as you know where we should camp in the wilderness, and you will be as eyes for us."* —Numbers 10:29, 31

Imagine the thrill in the camp! The cloud over the newly built tabernacle lifted. Silver trumpets signaled the muster. Banners raised. The tribes marched out. The people had camped at Sinai almost a year, but God was on the move again, and His people were following Him! The Law had been given, the tabernacle crafted, and the people organized and numbered. Now, the great journey to Canaan had begun. How far? Which direction? Where would they camp? All was in God's hands . . . supposedly. Moses had taken care to persuade his brother-in-law Hobab to accompany them, anxious for his help as a scout. Hobab was a Midianite; he knew the region and the locals. Were Moses's actions a hint that he was unsure of God's care for His people? How easily we give our concerns to God for His care only to snatch them back and try to work things out for ourselves.

Numbers 11

"Say to the people, 'Consecrate yourselves for tomorrow, and you shall eat meat; for you have wept in the ears of the LORD, saying, "Oh that someone would give us meat to eat! For we were well-off in Egypt." Therefore the LORD will give you meat and you shall eat.'"

—*Numbers 11:18*

Any parent who's undertaken a long journey knows it doesn't take long for the complaining to start. In Numbers, the riffraff among the people started it, but soon the Israelites joined in. Eventually, even Moses began complaining to God about their complaining! The bread provided from heaven was versatile and completely nourishing. But when seeds of ingratitude take root, they bear the fruit of selfish greed. When what God provides isn't enough, nothing will be enough. Manna seemed boring, even though it came from God's hand. Imagine that—being bored with God's plan and seeking after more elaborate and exciting things. The Israelites lamented for their Egyptian food, conveniently forgetting that they had eaten the Egyptians' fish and leeks as slaves. God gave the Israelites meat, enough to choke on and learn the lesson of quiet contentment. Let us all be careful with our petitions to God: are we actually scorning what He has already graciously provided?

Numbers 12

Then Miriam and Aaron spoke against Moses because of the Cushite woman whom he had married . . . and they said, "Has the Lord indeed spoken only through Moses? Has He not spoken through us as well?" And the Lord heard it. —*Numbers 12:1–2*

It was probably Miriam who waited by the reed bed on the Nile to intercede for her infant brother Moses (Exodus 2:4–8). She was also described as a prophetess in Exodus 15:20, leading the victory song after the Israelites crossed the Red Sea. She and Aaron were both older siblings to Moses, but Miriam likely led their complaint against Moses, because she is named first in Numbers 12 and bore the brunt of God's judgment for impudence. Miriam and Aaron's sibling rivalry toward Moses is expressed as a two-pronged attack—Moses had married a foreign woman, and he wasn't the only prophet in the camp. So why was he in charge? In reality, their questioning Moses's wife was a red herring; it was not forbidden to marry a Cushite. Miriam and Aaron's complaint boiled down to envy of their brother's authority. At some point, we, too, will face the temptation to covet someone else's position, rank, or privilege. May we learn not to let envy distort our priorities or cloud our thinking.

Numbers 13

Then Caleb quieted the people before Moses and said, "We should by all means go up and take possession of it, for we will surely overcome it." —*Numbers 13:30*

Caleb and Joshua were two of the twelve scouts sent out from Paran. On their return, they were the only ones who brought a confident report. The other spies painted a grim picture of defeat at the hands of giants. All the men had seen the same land, populated by the same people! How could the accounts have been so different? Attitude was the deciding factor. A negative attitude causes us to magnify obstacles and minimize our effectiveness. Pessimism invites paralysis. Caleb and Joshua were optimistic, because they knew that God was with them. They were eager to get on with His plan. Their courage had nothing to do with the fight being easy; it had everything to do with the sovereignty of their God. Sometimes we can look at the obstacles and let pessimism win out. When we do, we rob ourselves of the satisfaction of making a good effort for a good cause.

Numbers 14

"Surely all the men who have seen My glory and My signs which I performed in Egypt and in the wilderness, yet have put Me to the test these ten times and have not listened to My voice, shall by no means see the land which I swore to their fathers." —*Numbers 14:22–23*

It was the last straw: "Would that we had died in the land of Egypt!" (Numbers 14:2). Weak faith had given way to irrational fear. Only two years earlier, hard slavery had been the Israelites' portion. But at least they knew that world—the world of the whip. Their people had been in Egypt for four hundred years.

In all that time, God had not lost sight of them; in fact, the Israelites had prospered. Even more, He had heard their cries and delivered the people from a regime of oppression. But how quickly they forgot the lessons of the plagues in Egypt, the first Passover, and the parting of the Red Sea. They lost sight of God. Today, Christians take Communion, keep journals, and save mementos. The Bible calls such things "stones of help" (see 1 Samuel 7:12) — they help us remember. It's always a good idea to *remember* God's work in the past. It makes it easier to count on Him for the future.

Numbers 15

" 'As for the assembly, there shall be one statute for you and for the alien who sojourns with you, a perpetual statute throughout your generations; as you are, so shall the alien be before the LORD.' "

— Numbers 15:15

The failures of the first generation out of Egypt made it necessary to reiterate the covenant obligations to the new generation who would grow up in the wilderness while their parents dwindled away. Toward that end, God introduced the idea of an "in group" and an "out group." Interestingly, an Israelite could be factored in the "out group," and an alien could be factored in the "in group." National blessing was never fixed by genealogy; rather, blessing's boundary was porous and based on obedience. A person could choose to obey and be in the community of faith or to rebel and be excluded. A provision of forgiveness was to be made for unintentional sin, but intentional sin carried serious consequences. The same is true today — God accepts us based on our hearts, not our heritages. As Paul noted, Christ dismantled the barrier between Jews and Gentiles, making one new group from the two (Ephesians 2:13–22).

Numbers 16

But on the next day all the congregation of the sons of Israel grumbled against Moses and Aaron, saying, "You are the ones who have caused the death of the LORD's people." —*Numbers 16:41*

When Korah the Levite challenged Moses and Aaron for leadership of the Israelites, God's intention was clear and carried out swiftly. The earth swallowed up Korah and the rebels, while fire consumed the would-be-priests as they burned their incense. The people of Israel saw with their own eyes God's judgement against Korah. Yet remarkably, as soon as the next day, they blamed Moses and Aaron for the deaths of the rebels. Once spiritual blindness sets in, the old adage becomes plain: "There are none so blind as those who will not see." People who do not *accept* what they know to be *true* will try to dismantle that truth at all costs. We call it rationalization, and we often participate: "My wife doesn't understand me!" or "Everyone fudges on their expenses!" Let's not play games to justify selfish desires over God's plan. Let's open our eyes to truth.

Numbers 17

But the LORD said to Moses, "Put back the rod of Aaron before the testimony to be kept as a sign against the rebels, that you may put an end to their grumblings against Me, so that they will not die."

—*Numbers 17:10*

The people of Israel were shown, once and for all, that Moses and Aaron received their authority as high prophet and high priest from God Himself. The rod, or staff, was a symbol of authority. When Aaron's rod brought forth buds, blossoms, and almonds, it was a clear sign of his leadership. The rod didn't go back to

Aaron, however. The rebels' challenge cost them something, and a reminder of that fact would be close at hand for every Levite serving in the sanctuary. Aaron's rod was a memorial to a principle that had been clear throughout Israelite history since Abraham, Isaac, Jacob, and Joseph. God chooses whom He wills, and it is unwise to second-guess Him. For this reason, we should not be hasty but rather cautious and prayerful in establishing those who lead in our churches . . . and even more cautious should their leadership ever need to be challenged.

Numbers 18

So the LORD *said to Aaron, "You and your sons and your father's household with you shall bear the guilt in connection with the sanctuary, and you and your sons with you shall bear the guilt in connection with your priesthood."* —*Numbers 18:1*

With leadership and authority comes accountability. Aaron's priesthood had been vindicated, but the gravity of his office had to be made clear. His authority was not without limits, and his duties were carefully delineated. He was responsible for keeping the holy things holy and the profane things apart, on penalty of death. Numbers 18:1 came as solemn words to the man who had been famously, even comically, permissive during the incident of the golden calf: "So they gave [their gold] to me, and I threw it into the fire, and out came this calf" (Exodus 32:24). True leadership doesn't just mean making people do things; it means getting them to do the *right* things and helping them avoid the *wrong* things. Leadership without morality or ethics is mindless egotism. God held Aaron personally responsible for the caliber of his leadership, and it stands to reason the same holds true for God's leaders today.

Numbers 19

*"This is the statute of the law which the L*ORD *has commanded, saying, 'Speak to the sons of Israel that they bring you an unblemished red heifer in which is no defect and on which a yoke has never been placed.'"* —Numbers 19:2

The ashes of the red heifer had a special significance. They were the means by which those made unclean through the various events of life in the wilderness could purify themselves and reenter the camp. In particular, the ashes could be thought of as a kind of scrub that would remove the taint brought on by contact with corpses. Just as God instituted a clear line of distinction between the holy and the profane, He established a clear barrier between death and life. Death was outside, and life was inside the camp. The lesson is just as clear. Being inside the camp—in proximity to the Holy One—meant life for the faithful, who demonstrated their faith by observing God's prescriptions for approaching Him. Today, the symbolic cleansing provided by the red heifer has been supplanted by the ministry of Christ. No one approaches God—passes from death to life—except through Christ.

Numbers 20

Moses and Aaron gathered the assembly before the rock. And he said to them, "Listen now, you rebels; shall we bring forth water for you out of this rock?" —Numbers 20:10

Moses was exasperated. For four decades, he had dealt with this rebellious and ungrateful people. His frustration at their complaining over the dry spring at Kadesh was betrayed by his choice of words. Moses also intimated that it would be he and Aaron (not God) who would bring forth water for the people. Then with complete disregard for God's instructions, Moses struck the rock rather than speaking to it. His actions conveyed a false, dangerous message: Moses himself—not God—had provided the miraculous supply. Fatigue, annoyance, disappointment, frustration—it isn't always easy to work with people, even God's people. But God's response to Moses makes it clear: difficulties do not give us license to overstep our boundaries.

Numbers 21

Moses made a bronze serpent and set it on the standard; and it came about, that if a serpent bit any man, when he looked to the bronze serpent, he lived. —Numbers 21:9

Time and again, the Israelites had complained; time and again, God had preserved them and provided for them. The fiery snakes in the desert were an expression of His frustration. And the antidote for these snakes' particularly deadly bites was a curious one, involving looking up at a bronze serpent on a pole. The people's natural focus was on the problem—they frantically looked down, tending to bites and trying to avoid being bitten again. It wouldn't have made sense to think about looking up. But when they did, they shifted their focus from the problem to the cure God had provided, and they found relief. Speaking with Nicodemus, Jesus compared Himself to that bronze serpent in the wilderness, telling the old teacher that belief in Him was key (John 3:14–15). What was true for Nicodemus is true for us. It doesn't make sense to look up to the dying Man on the cross to find a cure for death. But that's where the cure lies.

Numbers 22

But God was angry because [Balaam] was going, and the angel of the
LORD took his stand in the way as an adversary against him.

—Numbers 22:22

What a puzzle was Balaam! He referred to God by God's personal
name, *JHWH*, the name revealed to Moses. And God spoke to
Balaam in plain terms as He did with Moses. From this, we can
deduce that Balaam was indeed a prophet of the one true God.
But history does not remember him well. Peter described Balaam
as one who "loved the wages of unrighteousness" (2 Peter 2:15).
His mercenary spirit ruled over his desire to obey God. Balaam's
spiritual services could be bought, even after God clearly told
him not to curse Israel (Numbers 22:12). In allowing Balaam to
go to Moab, God allowed the prophet to follow the evil desires of
his heart. But God sent opposition into Balaam's path. The world
says that everyone has their price. Some people are in ministry
for the money. But what good is it to gain the whole world and
yet allow God's favor to slip through our sticky fingers?

Numbers 23

"God is not a man, that He should lie,
Nor a son of man, that He should repent. . . .
Behold, I have received a command to bless;
When He has blessed, then I cannot revoke it."

—Numbers 23:19–20

Balak, the king of Moab, followed the diviner's elaborate instructions, building seven high altars and sacrificing seven rams and
bulls. But the prophet was under a strong constraint. The episode
of the talking donkey had made it plain that Balaam was dealing

with a force far beyond his power to control or manipulate (Numbers 22). In the past, spells and curses might have worked for him, calling perhaps on lesser spirits to work his schemes. But this time, seven *hundred* sacrifices would not have persuaded the Lord to change His mind. Balak was clearly in disbelief at the magician's inability to get his own way. *Perhaps a new vantage point could change the outcome?* Balak was grasping at straws, and Balaam was impotent before sovereign God. When God says it is so — it *will* be so. Twisting what He says or challenging the intent of what He decrees is an exercise in futility.

Numbers 24

"God brings him out of Egypt,
He is for him like the horns of the wild ox.
He will devour the nations who are his adversaries,
And will crush their bones in pieces,
And shatter them with his arrows."   — Numbers 24:8

From a third set of altars on a vantage point at Peor, Balaam surveyed the camp of Israel and finally recognized the futility of his attempts. Foregoing his omens and spells, he gazed out over the wilderness as he proclaimed an oracle of stunned and bewildered defeat. God had commandeered Balaam's spirit, and he was powerless to resist. It was clear to him now that Israel would succeed according to God's will. Balaam, famous for his powers, had become the celebrity proof that it was impossible to prevail against the one true God of Israel. Had the nations taken their cue from Balaam, they would not have resisted Israel when God's people approached the Promised Land. But characteristically, the nations were proud and stubborn, and they fell before the tribes of Jacob. It's important to remember that every knee will bow to the Lord in due time (Romans 14:10–12). Better it be in willing submission than in terrible defeat.

Numbers 25

While Israel remained at Shittim, the people began to play the harlot with the daughters of Moab. For they invited the people to the sacrifices of their gods, and the people ate and bowed down to their gods.
—*Numbers 25:1–2*

Balaam had prophesied that none could stand against the people of Israel because God was for them. Perhaps this knowledge caused Israel to lower its guard and drift into shameful ways. They were introduced to the worship of Baal, a mythical fertility god whose devotees believed their sexual exploits on earth would please Baal and induce him to make their land and their people fruitful. In today's terms, it was a cult that worshiped a pornographic voyeur. The one true God is not against sexuality, but He instituted marriage to be sexuality's arena and modesty to be the governing scruple outside that arena. God's reaction to the sleaze of Baalism was swift and deadly. The worship of sex, the perversion of its delights into voyeurism and public exhibitionism, is never going to be right in God's eyes. What we might glimpse on videos or the Internet isn't "personal indulgence"; it's a violation of God's divine design for sexual expression.

Numbers 26

But among these there was not a man of those who were numbered by Moses and Aaron the priest, who numbered the sons of Israel in the wilderness of Sinai. . . . And not a man was left of them, except Caleb the son of Jephunneh and Joshua the son of Nun.

— Numbers 26:64–65

The exiles out of Egypt had all died in the wilderness over the course of forty years. Only Caleb, Joshua, and Moses were left of those who had witnessed the plagues of Egypt, the first Passover, and the parting of the Red Sea. Another census was ordered by God to take stock and reveal what had been lost along the way in terms of man power. The results were surprising and encouraging. God had sustained His people as nomads in a harsh and barren place for four decades. Through all the complaints and setbacks, they had lost less than one third of one percent of their force. The new generation was almost exactly as numerous as the previous one. It's always in retrospect that we see God's provision. For that reason, we should take stock once in a while; we should pause and take a glance back. We must *remember* to *remind* ourselves of God's hand on our lives.

Numbers 27

Then the LORD spoke to Moses, saying, "The daughters of Zelophehad are right in their statements. You shall surely give them a hereditary possession among their father's brothers, and you shall transfer the inheritance of their father to them." — Numbers 27:6–7

The new census was directly associated with the allocation of tribal lands in the territory across the Jordan. One special case was brought before Moses. A "new generation" family was comprised of only daughters, and they feared that their father's tribal inheritance would be forfeited because they were women. Moses deferred to God as supreme magistrate and, without hesitation, added a divine caveat giving daughters land rights. This was a significant decision in a culture where women had few rights at all. Clearly, at that time, men (even righteous men) had not fully discerned God's plan for the way women and men were to cooperate in society. The fall had clouded the issue, and fallen men and women continue to compound the issue—an issue that only God can clarify. Men and women are of equal value in God's sight, however much we might differ in our roles and responsibilities.

Numbers 28

Then the LORD spoke to Moses, saying, "Command the sons of Israel and say to them, 'You shall be careful to present My offering, My food for My offerings by fire, of a soothing aroma to Me, at their appointed time.'"
—*Numbers 28:1–2*

We know that God doesn't physically need us to cook food for Him. So this is a strange prescription in many ways. Just like the census, the sacrifices were not for God's benefit but for Israel's. Through the sacrifices, God showed the new generation that each day, each week, each month, and each year they were to remember that everything they had when they settled in their new land—their flocks, herds, grains, and fruits—was given to them by God. The portion that they gave back to God was a lesson in tenancy. The owner of the field legitimately gets the first share. The ritual of sacrifice instilled in the people an ongoing sense of obligation. The resources were not theirs to begin with, but they were allowed to keep, use, and enjoy the vast majority of them. The same principle is helpful today. Let's use our borrowed resources with the real Owner in mind.

Numbers 29

"'Then on the fifteenth day of the seventh month you shall have a holy convocation; you shall do no laborious work, and you shall observe a feast to the LORD for seven days.'" —Numbers 29:12

The Israelite months and seasons can be a little confusing to modern-day Westerners, but they are extremely significant. The Feast of Tabernacles (Booths) was a week-long harvest festival that came to be known as the Great Feast and was surely the most exuberant of the festivals. At the time when Moses gave these instructions, the Feast of Tabernacles had never been celebrated. Up until then, temporary shelters were all this nomadic people had ever known. But once established in the Land of Promise, they would memorialize their wanderings by living in temporary booths for a week. Living in our earthly bodies, we, too, have only ever known temporary shelters. But we, too, have been given something to look forward to—something settled, something permanent.

Numbers 30

"If a man makes a vow to the LORD, or takes an oath to bind himself with a binding obligation, he shall not violate his word; he shall do according to all that proceeds out of his mouth." —Numbers 30:2

We would like to think that the ability and willingness to keep an obligation or to honor a promise is foundational to any just society. For this new generation of Israelites, however, it was important to reinforce the point. Their fathers had stood at the foot of Mount Horeb and proclaimed a vow: "All that the LORD has spoken we will do!" (Exodus 19:8). But they had followed that vow with challenges to Moses's leadership and Aaron's priesthood, as well as with doubts about the very idea that God would keep *His* promise to them. The old generation's failure was the result of a low regard for promises. The principle of promise-keeping is at the heart of all relationships. In our marriages and our finances, in our commitments and civic duties, Christians should be known for keeping promises. God is a keeper of promises, and His people should be people of their word.

Numbers 31

"Take full vengeance for the sons of Israel on the Midianites; afterward you will be gathered to your people." Moses spoke to the people, saying, "Arm men from among you for the war, that they may go against Midian to execute the LORD's vengeance on Midian."

— Numbers 31:2–3

The stakes were high on the plains of Moab. Israel could already see their land, just across the Jordan. If they were to succeed, their devotion to God had to be purged of the alloy of paganism. They had to learn — and learn quickly — that there is a way that might seem attractive, but it leads to death (Proverbs 14:12). Notice the contrast between how the narrative deals with the lives of the Midianites (the tribe who had beguiled nearly all of Israel into Baal worship) and the life of Moses, God's faithful prophet: "Deal definitively with Midian's attempted seduction and then come home to Me" is the essence of what God said to Moses. To die as God's friend or to die as His enemy are really the only two choices available to any of us. What happens after the event will all be determined by what we have believed before it.

Numbers 32

"If the sons of Gad and the sons of Reuben, everyone who is armed for battle, will cross with you over the Jordan in the presence of the Lord, *and the land is subdued before you, then you shall give them the land of Gilead for a possession."*   —*Numbers 32:29*

As a matter of natural ability and preference, cattle are more at home on flat pasture, while sheep and goats do well on hilly terrain. The tribes of Reuben and Gad had become specialists in raising cattle. To these men, the land where they stood looked a lot more suitable for running large herds than the craggy land across the river. Moses immediately challenged the motive behind their petition to stay. Were they trying to stay safely out of the fight that awaited them? Their quick answer was brave and sincere. Not only would they fight, but they would take point duty until the land was settled. The notion of, *What's best for me?* did not eclipse the question of, *What's best for the community?* In the end, what's best for the community (in our case, the church universal) will prove to be what's best for us in the long run as well.

Numbers 33

" 'But if you do not drive out the inhabitants of the land from before you, then it shall come about that those whom you let remain of them will become as pricks in your eyes and as thorns in your sides, and they will trouble you in the land in which you live.' "

—*Numbers 33:55*

More than a half-millennium before this declaration was made, God had given this land to Abraham. Dwarfed by its neighbors in the region and subject to the ebb and flow of the tides of vast empires, Israel's tiny patch of real estate was to be a lighthouse.

The land was to be a fixed place where God's perfect will would be administered; where justice, grace, and mercy would be found; and where the nations would see the wisdom of following the one true God. As such, Canaan was to be made a truly holy land. Painters know it only takes a hint of carmine to pollute a palette of white, and no amount of additional white will take away the hue. The same principle applied in Canaan and continues today. God is constantly in the process of making things pure, of reversing the pollution of sin. We can cooperate or resist, join the enterprise or reject it, but eventually, it will be done.

Numbers 34

Then the LORD spoke to Moses, saying, "Command the sons of Israel and say to them, 'When you enter the land of Canaan, this is the land that shall fall to you as an inheritance, even the land of Canaan according to its borders.'" —Numbers 34:1–2

God did not give the Israelites unlimited sway. Their places were fixed, predetermined in God's plan for them. They would never command vast empires as did the Persians, Greeks, and Romans. That wasn't the Israelites' role. Their geographical places were modest; their political places were limited. It was their *theological* place that was so very crucial. A small country with a boundless God! Within their narrow borders, there was to be a nation that the greatest of monarchs would marvel. We see glimpses of this in such moments as the visit of the Queen of Sheba to Solomon's court. She traveled perhaps a thousand miles to see what real wisdom looked like (1 Kings 10:1–10). The question for us today: how are we doing at remaining holy in the small places we've been given? Can we keep our boundaries and yet shine a divine light? Will we speak with absolute confidence about His wisdom, grace, and mercy?

Numbers 35

"'The cities shall be to you as a refuge from the avenger, so that the manslayer will not die until he stands before the congregation for trial. The cities which you are to give shall be your six cities of refuge.'" —Numbers 35:12–13

When left to the court of personal opinion, justice is always a tricky problem. The temptation is to exact vengeance first and ask questions later. Behind any blood-crime there exist mitigating circumstances and reasonable doubts. Without God's clarity of vision, that will always be the case. God, who knows humankind's ways, wants all prejudices and vendettas to be quenched and all reasons and justifications to be heard. Therefore, He established cities of sanctuary for the Israelites, where the targets of vendettas could receive fair hearings and explain their cases. This is the foundational basis of *habeas corpus*, the legal bedrock upon which the Magna Carta and subsequently the American Constitution were built. Is it not fair to say that God's ways are eternal? Justice did not spring up as an invention of humanity; it has always been in the mind of God.

Numbers 36

These are the commandments and the ordinances which the Lord commanded to the sons of Israel through Moses in the plains of Moab by the Jordan opposite Jericho. —Numbers 36:13

Not every particular contingency of law could be encompassed by the Law given to Israel for life in Canaan. Nevertheless, the principal matters of justice and righteousness could be deduced from what God gave to His people, through Moses, as they prepared to cross the Jordan. The book of Numbers explains why the first exiles out of Egypt never found their victory. They could have been in the Promised Land within two years of their release from slavery, but instead they listened to naysayers. The book of Numbers explains the high stakes involved in the establishment of a holy land—if they muddled their worship of the one true God, they would perish. And the book of Numbers says to us that God is very serious about our dedication to Him, our respect for His ways, and His constant, gracious watch over our own journeys.

Deuteronomy

Deuteronomy 1

"'See, the LORD your God has placed the land before you; go up, take possession, as the LORD, the God of your fathers, has spoken to you. Do not fear or be dismayed.'" —*Deuteronomy 1:21*

Grumbling, moaning, and disobedient, the people of Israel proved their lack of faith in God's promise. When the LORD rescued His people from Egyptian slavery, they complained. When He led them to the boundary of their lavish land, they retreated. Even though God sheltered them by day and warmed them by night, they didn't trust Him. Deuteronomy 1 recalls God's relationship with His people as they trekked to Canaan. Although the Israelites didn't enter the land initially, they did eventually. And they will again—eternally—because of God's faithfulness to His covenant with Abraham. Christians also have an eternal home He has promised to us. When God leads you to a difficult job, financial stress, or a crossroad in life, do you complain? When storms hit and life takes a chaotic turn, do you put your hope in eternity? Let's throw off the worries that weigh us down and trust Christ.

Deuteronomy 2

"'This day I will begin to put the dread and fear of you upon the peoples everywhere under the heavens, who, when they hear the report of you, will tremble and be in anguish because of you.'"
—*Deuteronomy 2:25*

When God commanded His people to march against Sihon, King of Heshbon, did He expect them to fight with military prowess alone? No. God not only equipped the children of Israel for battle, He also prepared their enemies. He filled the army of King

Sihon with dread—the fear of death. Now, God may not place terror in the hearts of our mean coworkers and crazy in-laws. But we can trust that He will sovereignly work in their lives in order to accomplish His will. When we face conflict, do we desperately work to defend ourselves, taking matters into our own hands? Or do we entrust ourselves to God's perfect plan as He directs the hearts of our "enemies"? The Lord may not defeat our foes before our eyes, but He powerfully works in all circumstances to achieve His good will (Romans 8:28–35).

Deuteronomy 3

"But the LORD was angry with me on your account, and would not listen to me; and the LORD said to me, 'Enough! Speak to Me no more of this matter.'"   —Deuteronomy 3:26

Sometimes God says no. We pray diligently—begging God to grant a request—but He denies our heart's desire. How do we respond? Do we pout and ignore Him? Moses asked God earnestly to allow him to enter the Promised Land, but God said no. Why? While God's parched people journeyed to their new home, He planned to give them miraculous water. He told Moses to speak to the rock at Meribah and command the nourishing river to break forth. But Moses disobeyed and smacked the rock with his staff. As a result, God disciplined Moses and swore he wouldn't set foot in the Promised Land. Even though Moses pleaded, God kept His word. We don't always know why God answers no. But we do know that He is a faithful Father.

> For whom the LORD loves He reproves
> Even as a father corrects the son in whom
>   he delights.   (Proverbs 3:12)

Deuteronomy 4

"There you will serve gods, the work of man's hands, wood and stone, which neither see nor hear nor eat nor smell. But from there you will seek the LORD your God, and you will find Him if you search for Him with all your heart and all your soul." — *Deuteronomy 4:28–29*

God's mercy extends from east to west, from eternity past to eternity future. As the Lord prepared the people of Israel to enter the land of promise, He knew they would fail. But God also knew that after they embraced idolatry and received their punishment, they would seek Him — and He vowed to forgive them. Fast forward about eight hundred years. With most of the children of Israel exiled in Babylon as a consequence of sin, the prophet Jeremiah implored the people to seek God's forgiveness and believe in His coming deliverance (see Jeremiah 29:13–14). Similarly, when Christians today violate God's Word and receive His discipline, we should seek His forgiveness with a pure heart. He wants us to pursue His grace, through faith in Jesus Christ. "Therefore let us draw near with confidence to the throne of grace, so that we may receive mercy and find grace to help in time of need" (Hebrews 4:16).

Deuteronomy 5

" 'I am the LORD your God who brought you out of the land of Egypt, out of the house of slavery.' "—*Deuteronomy 5:6*

God rescues. He chose Abraham and created a people—Israel—who would display God's character to the nations. He redeemed His people from Egyptian bondage and brought them to the boundary of their new home. Deuteronomy 5:6 introduces the Ten Commandments—the guidelines for Israel's interaction with God and people. God's redemption forms the foundation of His covenant relationship with the people of Israel. God acted first, in grace, and He called the Israelites to obey in response. As Christians, we don't follow God's rules to earn His approval. We obey God out of gratitude for salvation. We obey by means of the Holy Spirit, not by willpower. Just as God chose Abraham while he was a pagan, Jesus Christ died for us in the midst of our rebellion. God's saving work on our behalf should motivate us to submit to His Word and display His grace to others (see Romans 5:8).

Deuteronomy 6

"O Israel, you should listen and be careful to [keep God's command-ments], that it may be well with you and that you may multiply greatly, just as the LORD, the God of your fathers, has promised you, in a land flowing with milk and honey." — *Deuteronomy 6:3*

God provided His people with a land full of amenities. In their new home, the people of Israel didn't have to dig wells, water the land, clear fields, or build houses. But they did have to stew-ard the gifts God had given them. The Promised Land belonged to God, not Israel. The Lord warned the Israelites not to forget Him when they entered a land with abundant food, shelter, and beauty (Deuteronomy 6:12). He reminded them that His blessing was connected to their obedience. When Christians have enough stuff, we tend to forget God. We get spiritual amnesia and neglect God's Word. Christians often forget God's provision and that all things belong to Him. So how can we remember God's universal ownership and generosity? We must consciously live as stewards of His resources every day. This will prompt us to rely on Him, seek His guidance, and generously share His gifts with others.

Deuteronomy 7

*"You shall tear down their altars, and smash their sacred pillars . . .
For you are a holy people to the LORD your God; the LORD your God
has chosen you to be a people for His own possession out of all the
peoples who are on the face of the earth."*   —*Deuteronomy 7:5–6*

Be holy—distinct from your culture. When the people of Israel
entered the land, God told them to clean house by removing all
vestiges of idolatry. The one true God wanted to reside among
His people. And since He is holy, His people had to lead holy
lives. God wanted Israel to shine like a beacon of light to the
nations. Their unique worship of the LORD and their adherence to
His Law set them apart. We, as Christians, must be different from
our neighbors. We are to live and think according to a new standard (Romans 12:1–2). We should love unconditionally, forgive
freely, give generously, and obey God fearlessly. While we may
not cling to idols of stone and wood, we must examine our lives
and destroy anything that we worship in place of God—money,
prestige, comfort. Why? The Lord intends to draw others to Him
through us.

Deuteronomy 8

*"[God] humbled you and let you be hungry, and fed you with manna
which you did not know . . . that He might make you understand that
man does not live by bread alone, but man lives by everything that
proceeds out of the mouth of the LORD."*   —*Deuteronomy 8:3*

Food and water sustain our physical existence. But what
nourishes our spiritual appetite? What can't we live without?
Deuteronomy 8 proves that human beings waste away unless we

feed on God's Word. God gave physical food—manna—to the Israelites. But before He fed His people in the desert, He allowed their stomachs to growl. They cried out to Him, their provider, to give them something to eat. God taught them that He provides not only sustenance to their bodies but spiritual food—His Word. In their physical hunger, they realized their complete dependence on God for spiritual provision. In Deuteronomy 8, God recalled His provision for His people and warned them not to forget Him when they entered their new land and lacked nothing (Deuteronomy 8:11–14). When Christians today have little need of physical provision, we often forget our spiritual need for God. Remember! Only God's Word can satisfy your spiritual appetite.

Deuteronomy 9

"I prayed to the LORD and said, 'O Lord God, do not destroy Your people, even Your inheritance, whom You have redeemed through Your greatness, whom You have brought out of Egypt with a mighty hand.'" —*Deuteronomy 9:26*

Deuteronomy 9 recounts Israel's rebellion in spite of God's provision and faithfulness to His covenant. When Aaron led the people in an idolatrous building project, God put His foot down. He intended to destroy Aaron and all of Israel, but Moses interceded. After Moses's outburst of anger toward the people, in which he destroyed the tablets of the Ten Commandments, he prayed. For forty days and nights, Moses lay prostrate before God and begged Him to show mercy (Exodus 32:11–13). And God answered his prayer. Moses modeled the Christian response to encountering disobedience and immorality within the church and outside — pray! In humility, we should plead with God for justice and mercy. So the next time you get upset at the latest celebrity infidelity or church scandal, don't gossip. Instead, pray. "Therefore, confess your sins to one another, and pray for one another so that you may be healed" (James 5:16).

Deuteronomy 10

At that time the LORD set apart the tribe of Levi to carry the ark of the covenant of the LORD, to stand before the LORD to serve Him and to bless in His name until this day.   *— Deuteronomy 10:8*

The ark of the covenant was heavy! Made of acacia wood and covered with gold, it took several men to lug it from place to place. The Levites, the ones God entrusted with caring for the ark, must have burned more than a few extra calories as Israel traveled to new destinations. This task might seem mundane, but to transport the very dwelling place of God was actually the most important job of all. To think that the Holy God of the universe was present there among His people must have scared the sandals off the Levites. But does this truth fill Christians today with reverence? God still dwells among His people — in each believer individually and in the church as a whole. May we Christians care for the temple of the Lord with as much devotion and reverence as the Levites cared for the ark of the covenant.

Deuteronomy 11

"You shall therefore impress these words of mine on your heart and on your soul; and you shall bind them as a sign on your hand, and they shall be as frontals on your forehead." — *Deuteronomy 11:18*

God instructed the Israelites to teach His commandments so that the younger generation, which didn't witness the plagues or wilderness miracles, would know, worship, and obey Him. God described the spirit in which His people should teach His Law to the next generation — by binding His Words on their hands and wearing them as frontals on their foreheads. But what does this mean? Frontals were decorative headbands worn in the ancient Near East. Jews later created phylacteries — small, black boxes that held Scriptures written on parchment — which they wore on their foreheads and left arms.[2] They took God's command in Deuteronomy 11 literally, but God wanted Israel to ingrain His Law on their minds and obey Him with their actions. God requires obedience that flows from a mind fixed on His Word and deeds inspired by love for Him. May we Christians obey God wholeheartedly and teach our children to do the same.

Deuteronomy 12

"Whatever I command you, you shall be careful to do; you shall not add to nor take away from it." — *Deuteronomy 12:32*

Habakkuk, Philemon, and Obadiah. Sometimes these books lay untouched on our shelves — lonely, neglected, and dusty. We often value certain parts of the Bible more than others. When we do so, we may be altering God's Word, at least in our hearts. In Deuteronomy 12, God commanded the Israelites to observe everything written in His Law so that they would experience His blessing. God would dwell among them in His future Temple, but only if they maintained purity. In order for God's people to obey His Law, they had to know it. He charged fathers to teach the Law to their children and weave His words into the fabric of their lives (Deuteronomy 6:6–9). If the people ignored part of His Law, God would discipline them. And if Christians today ignore books in the Bible because they seem irrelevant, God will not approve. We will risk "taking away" part of His inerrant Word.

Deuteronomy 13

"Nothing from that which is put under the ban shall cling to your hand, in order that the LORD may turn from His burning anger and show mercy to you, and have compassion on you and make you increase, just as He has sworn to your fathers."

—Deuteronomy 13:17

God doesn't take idolatry lightly. If several witnesses testified that an Israelite had bowed down to another god, that person received swift punishment—death! When the Israelites invaded a foreign land, God allowed them to keep the treasures of the land as booty. But when idolatry existed in one of the Israelite cities, God commanded His people to kill all the inhabitants and set fire to everything as a burnt offering to Him. Traditionally, a burnt offering signified the end of a period of cleansing (Leviticus 12:6–8; 14:19–20; 15:14–15), so burning the city showed that the

Israelites had cleansed it of idolatry. How seriously do Christians take the worship of false gods? Western culture has established materialism and comfort as deities worthy of worship. Often Christians buy into this lie. How can our lives demonstrate that we worship the one true God alone? What do we need to "burn" today?

Deuteronomy 14

"At the end of every third year you shall bring out all the tithe of your produce in that year . . . The Levite, because he has no portion or inheritance among you, and the alien, the orphan and the widow who are in your town, shall come and eat and be satisfied."

—*Deuteronomy 14:28–29*

What sets God's people apart from our neighbors? In part, it's the way we satisfy our cravings and spend our money. Deuteronomy 14 reminds Israel about clean and unclean animals and the importance of the tithe. Whenever the Israelites ate a meal, they thought of God. Was dinner clean or unclean? And every time they harvested, they thought of God. In order to give God the right tithe each year, they had to keep track of the produce they reaped. And every third year, they thought of those without land or an inheritance — Levites, aliens, orphans, and widows. God's people shone like a light on a dark, foggy night when they followed His Law. Christians, likewise, should honor Him by the way we satisfy our cravings. We should rely on Him when we receive our paychecks. And we should develop generosity as we share with those in need. If we live like this, people will notice.

Deuteronomy 15

"Beware that there is no base thought in your heart, saying, 'The seventh year, the year of remission, is near,' and your eye is hostile toward your poor brother, and you give him nothing; then he may cry to the LORD against you, and it will be a sin in you."

—*Deuteronomy 15:9*

God tests the heart — often by checking our pocketbook. The treasure we accumulate for ourselves reveals the condition of our hearts. Every seventh year, God commanded His people to forgive debts owed by fellow Israelites. This worked out great if someone loaned money to a prosperous brother and received payment for seven years. But what if a poor brother, without means to repay, sought a loan halfway through the sixth year? An Israelite in this position could hope for very little repayment, only to forgive the debt in a few months. The savvy businessman wouldn't lend to the poor person but God prohibited this discrimination. He expected the Israelites, who had received everything from Him, to lend freely to poor and rich alike. Similarly, all that we have God has given to us. He expects us to share His gifts with others. Tightfisted Christians aren't displaying God's generous character.

Deuteronomy 16

"Three times in a year all your males shall appear before the LORD your God in the place which He chooses, at the Feast of Unleavened Bread and at the Feast of Weeks and at the Feast of Booths, and they shall not appear before the LORD empty-handed."

—*Deuteronomy 16:16*

God doesn't desire wooden ritualism, but loving worship. He established festivals to remind the Israelites of His gracious character. They observed the Passover (Feast of Unleavened Bread), a weeklong feast, to recall the exodus from Egypt. Seven weeks later, they held the Feast of Weeks and sacrificed freewill offerings to God to commemorate His deliverance and His Law. Then, seven days after harvest, the Israelites celebrated the Feast of Booths—a joyful week of gratitude for God's provision. At each festival, the people brought an offering to the Lord based on the blessing God had given them. Gratitude should motivate our obedience to God. In order to develop thankful hearts, Christians must recall God's work in our lives. Like the Israelites, we should set up memorials to remember God's grace and provision. We can celebrate the anniversary of our salvation, tithe regularly, serve at church, and keep a journal of answered prayer.

Deuteronomy 17

"When you enter the land which the Lord your God gives you, and you possess it and live in it, and you say, 'I will set a king over me like all the nations who are around me,' you shall surely set a king over you whom the Lord your God chooses."

—Deuteronomy 17:14–15

God ruled as king over Israel, and He intended to remain its monarch. Only He can govern with perfect justice, love, and power. But the people of Israel had wandering eyes. Instead of focusing on God, the people tried to fit in with the surrounding nations—all of which had human kings. God warned the Israelites that they would regret their decision to reject God as king. Human rulers exhibit injustice, selfishness, and moral weakness. But Israel demanded a human king anyway. God graciously granted their wish and established Saul as their first monarch (see 1 Samuel 8). Saul showed promise but eventually succumbed to fear and embraced disobedience. Will we, as Christians, accept God's rule in our lives, or will we set up ourselves as sovereign? The only one worthy of the title "king" has gained victory over sin and death and advocates for Christians at the Father's right hand. Will you bow to Jesus today?

Deuteronomy 18

"The Levitical priests, the whole tribe of Levi, shall have no portion or inheritance with Israel; they shall eat the LORD's offerings by fire and His portion. They shall have no inheritance among their countrymen; the LORD is their inheritance, as He promised them."

—Deuteronomy 18:1–2

The Levites were homeless. They received no permanent land on which to plant, harvest, or build homes. In return for their service in God's house, they received the tithes of Israel as their provision. The Levitical priests depended on the obedience of Israel, and ultimately on God, to meet their daily needs. The other tribes willed their land to future generations. But the Levites had a spiritual inheritance — God Himself. God rewarded their service with His presence. Christians should follow the example of the Levites who had to trust God to supply everything they needed. The New Testament calls followers of Christ "a chosen race, a royal priesthood, a holy nation, a people for God's own possession" (1 Peter 2:9). God has not given Christians a permanent inheritance on this earth, but He will give us an everlasting home on the new earth — and God Himself will be our reward (1 Peter 1:3–5).

Deuteronomy 19

"Now this is the case of the manslayer who may flee there and live: when he kills his friend unintentionally, not hating him previously."
— *Deuteronomy 19:4*

Moses instructed the Israelites to establish three cities of refuge after they crossed the Jordan. God told His people to protect anyone who killed another person accidentally by allowing the killer to escape to these cities. He did this so that a close relative of the deceased person wouldn't avenge the death by murdering the unintentional killer. When the manslayer arrived in the city of refuge, the elders were obligated to protect him. God's provision of these cities shows that He offers refuge for His people. So how should Christians live in light of this truth? The psalmist encouraged us to approach God with our cares, concerns, and secret sin — trusting that Christ has covered all transgressions.

> Trust in Him at all times, O people;
> Pour out your heart before Him;
> God is a refuge for us. (Psalm 62:8)

Deuteronomy 20

*"He shall say to them, 'Hear, O Israel, you are approaching the battle against your enemies today . . Do not be afraid, or panic, or tremble before them, for the L*ORD *your God is the one who goes with you, to fight for you against your enemies, to save you.'"*
— *Deuteronomy 20:3–4*

The Levitical priests played a central role in war. They carried the ark of the covenant, which represented God's presence, onto the battlefield. They also taught the people about God's character. When the Israelites marched against an enemy, the priests reminded them not to fear and encouraged them to trust in God's protection. The priests recalled God's promises and Moses's words: "Do not fear them, for the LORD your God is the one fighting for you" (Deuteronomy 3:22). When the soldiers embraced fear, their faith in God faded. God protects Christians today just like He protected Israel. But Christians do not battle against human enemies, and we don't use physical weapons (2 Corinthians 10:4). Followers of Christ use God's Word to war against Satan and his demons who seek to derail our journeys with God. Jesus Christ has overcome these evil powers, and He has given Christians victory over death (Colossians 2:15).

Deuteronomy 21

"But he shall acknowledge the firstborn, the son of the unloved, by giving him a double portion of all that he has, for he is the beginning of his strength; to him belongs the right of the firstborn."

—*Deuteronomy 21:17*

God hates favoritism—especially when it sinks the downtrodden deeper into despair. He established laws to protect the widow, orphan, and alien. In Deuteronomy 21:17, He proved His care for the rejected son of a man's unloved wife. If a man had multiple wives, he often loved one more than the other. In this case, the man might not give the double inheritance to his firstborn son if he was born to the unloved wife. But God prohibited this type of discrimination. So, when you go to a social gathering, will you confine your conversation to your peers—those who make similar livings, drive similar cars, and live in similar neighborhoods? Or will you associate with people you view as below your social class, treating them with equal respect, humility, and friendliness? Christians should value people as God does—all people have inherent worth, deserve love, and need grace.

Deuteronomy 22

"You shall not see your countryman's donkey or his ox fallen down on the way, and pay no attention to them; you shall certainly help him to raise them up." — Deuteronomy 22:4

It's not exactly easy to pick up an ox or a donkey. But if an Israelite saw his neighbor's animal lying on the side of the road, God expected him to help. It would take time, strength, and inconvenience to transport the animal back to its owner. And God required the Israelites to pay what it cost to help their countryman, especially since the ox and the donkey signified the core of a person's wealth in the ancient world. God cares about the interests of His people. He extends grace, answers prayer, and liberally blesses them. Just as God loves His people and provides for them, Christians should likewise sacrifice time and wealth to help one another. We should act like good neighbors and assist our brothers and sisters in need. Just like the Good Samaritan (Luke 10:30–37), we should consider the needs of others as more important than our own.

Deuteronomy 23

"Since the LORD your God walks in the midst of your camp to deliver you and to defeat your enemies before you, therefore your camp must be holy; and He must not see anything indecent among you or He will turn away from you." — Deuteronomy 23:14

God cares about purity. He can't live among a polluted people. God's Law prescribed detailed methods of physical purification for the Israelites. But cleanliness also extended to financial issues, making vows to God, and stealing from one another. In Deuteronomy 23, God prohibited the Israelites from exacting interest on loans given to their brothers, harvesting a neighbor's crops, and neglecting their promises to God. God is holy and He requires holiness from His people. God's character should inspire Christians to pursue godliness. His desire to live among us should lead to undefiled worship. Through Jesus Christ, believers have received righteousness and purity. But that doesn't mean that we should cheapen His grace by living polluted lives. If God spent a day with you, what would He smell? Would the foul odors of selfish ambition and lies displease Him? Or would the fragrance of humility, love, and worship make Him feel at home?

Deuteronomy 24

"When you reap your harvest in your field and have forgotten a sheaf in the field, you shall not go back to get it; it shall be for the alien, for the orphan, and for the widow, in order that the LORD your God may bless you in all the work of your hands."

—*Deuteronomy 24:19*

When you get your paycheck, do you already have plans to spend it all on yourself? Or do you intend to share some with the less fortunate in your community? God cares about the poor and outcast, and He expects His people to provide for them. He abundantly blessed Israel. God commanded His people to gather their grain, olives, and grapes from the field once and then leave the rest for the alien, widow, orphan, and impoverished. He wanted the Israelites to remember that they had lived as poor slaves in Egypt. God redeemed them and provided everything they needed. They faced the danger of forgetfulness when they entered the abundant Promised Land. And when they forgot their dependence on God, they disobeyed Him. God also expects Christians to share God's gifts with others. Remember! We, too, were slaves to sin but God redeemed us and provides everything we have.

Deuteronomy 25

"You shall have a full and just weight; you shall have a full and just measure, that your days may be prolonged in the land which the LORD *your God gives you."* — *Deuteronomy 25:15*

Dishonesty among God's people tarnishes His name. When the Israelites bought or sold items from each other, they used scales to measure the goods. They placed an item for sale on one side of the scale and measured it according to a standard weight on the other side. But sometimes, in order to cheat a person out of some grain or oil, a deceitful Israelite used an incorrect weight to measure the product. This trickery violated God's just character and warranted His discipline. God had promised to bless the people of Israel abundantly when they obeyed Him. So, ultimately, this duplicitous behavior revealed a lack of trust in God's ability to provide. A cheater with unjust weights denied God's promise and reaped His anger. Christians also depend on God for daily provision. Our dishonesty displays pride, self-reliance, and lack of faith in Him.

Deuteronomy 26

"Look down from Your holy habitation, from heaven, and bless Your people Israel, and the ground which You have given us, a land flowing with milk and honey, as You swore to our fathers."

—Deuteronomy 26:15

Should we ask God to bless us? Doesn't that seem prideful? Deuteronomy 26:15 concludes a liturgy on tithing with a prayer: *God, please bless your people.* After the Israelites had entered their new home, God told them to share a portion of their produce with the Levite, alien, fatherless, and widow. After giving their tithe, they repeated a prayer recalling their redemption from Egypt and God's promise to give them a permanent land. This prayer reinforced Israel's faith in God's eternal covenant and His promise to provide for them. And after following the Law and giving their tithe, they asked for His blessing. As Christians, we do not follow the Mosaic Law, so monetary blessing doesn't necessarily follow from obedience. But we should recognize God's provision and promises to us. Our heavenly Father loves us and has already given us every spiritual blessing in Jesus Christ. Let's thank Him for His blessing!

Deuteronomy 27

" 'Cursed is he who does not confirm the words of this law by doing them.' And all the people shall say, 'Amen.' "

—Deuteronomy 27:26

Actions speak louder than words. Want to prove the content of your heart? Show it! How does your spouse respond when you take out the trash or wash the dishes with a bad attitude? Heartfelt service shows our love—empty ritualism does not.

Deuteronomy 27 lists lots of curses for disobeying God's Law. But God wanted more than outward obedience—He longed for His people to love Him and manifest His character to the surrounding nations. God chose Israel so that He would have a representative on earth. The unique laws of God's people confirmed that they had a unique God. Not much has changed. Jesus Christ calls Christians to an obedience that illustrates a changed heart and a new allegiance. Ultimately, obedience to God shows our love for Him, and it demonstrates His character to our culture. "If you love Me, you will keep My commandments" (John 14:15).

Deuteronomy 28

"So your life shall hang in doubt before you; and you will be in dread night and day, and you shall have no assurance of your life."

—*Deuteronomy 28:66*

Life without God introduces chaos, fear, and despair. Even believers who rely on their own wisdom and rebel against God often lead miserable lives. Deuteronomy 28 outlines the curses God promised to send on His people if they disobeyed Him. After all He had done for the people of Israel—choosing, redeeming, and blessing them—God knew they would forget Him. While the long list of curses in Deuteronomy seems cruel, it actually shows God's grace. He disciplined His people so they would remember Him and repent. When His people deserted Him to chase idols, God scattered them among idolatrous nations. These savage nations reminded Israel of God's love. Since Christians don't live under the Mosaic Law, we don't have to fear reaping these curses for disobedience. But God does discipline us when we forget Him. In grace, God draws us back to Him by reminding us that we need Him.

Deuteronomy 29

"It shall be when he hears the words of this curse, that he will boast, saying, 'I have peace though I walk in the stubbornness of my heart in order to destroy the watered land with the dry.'"

—*Deuteronomy 29:19*

Do you take God's grace for granted? Do you expect His favor while you pursue your selfish desires? When an Israelite worshiped false gods but also invoked God's blessing because he or she belonged to God's covenant people, God pronounced that person cursed. Deuteronomy 29 recounts the renewal of the Mosaic Covenant, which God established with Israel at Horeb. In this chapter, Moses wrote about God's miraculous deliverance and His provision of clothes that didn't wear out for forty years. God defeated Israel's enemies and brought His people to their new home. As a result, He wanted the Israelites to follow His commandments from their hearts. But the Israelite who kept the form of the Law while living in sin mocked God's mercy. Do we expect God's blessing because we call ourselves Christians, even though we pursue our own will? Christ calls us to surrender, because God's grace has delivered us from sin and death.

Deuteronomy 30

"Then the Lord *your God will restore you from captivity, and have compassion on you, and will gather you again from all the peoples where the* Lord *your God has scattered you."* —*Deuteronomy 30:3*

God foretold a time when He would deport Israel to foreign lands because of their sin. But He also promised to restore His people to the Promised Land after they repented and sought His forgiveness. In 722 BC, Assyria captured the ten tribes of the northern kingdom and carried them away. In 586 BC, Babylon invaded Jerusalem and took the two tribes of the southern kingdom. Later, the Persian king, Cyrus, allowed the Jews to go back to their land. Will God ultimately finish gathering all of the Israelites from captivity? We know from Scripture that God keeps His promises. God will keep His covenant and will once again show mercy by returning all of Israel to the land (Ezekiel 37:21–22). But until that happens, Christians should pray for Israel—that they would believe in the Messiah, Jesus Christ.

Deuteronomy 31

"Assemble the people, the men and the women and children and the alien who is in your town, so that they may hear and learn and fear the LORD your God, and be careful to observe all the words of this law." —*Deuteronomy 31:12*

As Moses prepared Israel for his death and Joshua's leadership, he commanded the priests to read God's Law to the people every seven years during the Feast of Tabernacles. During this sabbatical year, God's people cancelled debts and gave the land rest from planting and harvesting. During the Feast of Tabernacles, they recalled God's deliverance from Egyptian bondage and celebrated His blessings. As the priests read God's Law, they taught the people—especially the children—to fear God and to obey His commands. The Israelite children didn't experience God's miraculous provision in the wilderness, so this public reading explained their people's history and God's covenant. How often does your church read Scripture out loud, as a congregation? God's Word has the power to transform lives. Do you spend time reading the Bible with your family? What a significant way to commit yourself to Scripture as a community and as a family.

Deuteronomy 32

"But Jeshurun grew fat and kicked—
You are grown fat, thick, and sleek—
Then he forsook God who made him,
And scorned the Rock of his salvation."   —*Deuteronomy 32:15*

How do we feel when we've eaten too much? Full, tired, and cranky. When the Israelites received the abundant food, drink, homes, and wealth God had given them, they grew fat, lazy, and obstinate. With a touch of irony, God called His people Jeshurun, meaning "upright people." Though many Israelites were once righteous, they became wicked. First, they enjoyed God's gifts—but they didn't thank Him. Next, they overindulged, failing to exercise self-control. Finally, after taking credit for their wealth and living hedonistic lives, they "kicked" against God—they revolted against His Law. As a result, they left Him and followed idols. As Christians, gratitude, restraint, and worship protect us from recalcitrance. By faith, we have received Jesus Christ's righteousness, but we don't always act that way. We must ask, *Have I eaten too much without giving thanks? Have I grown fat, wealthy, and prideful?* We can return to God, seeking His forgiveness.

Deuteronomy 33

"Blessed are you, O Israel;
Who is like you, a people saved by the L<small>ORD</small>,
Who is the shield of your help
And the sword of your majesty!
So your enemies will cringe before you,
And you will tread upon their high places."   *—Deuteronomy 33:29*

Are the most well-off people in the world those with prominent jobs, luxury cars, huge 401(k)s, loving families, and good health? Or are Christians the most "well-off"—even if we don't have all those things? Moses called the people of Israel blessed, not only because God promised to reward them for their obedience, but because the Lord was their God. God gives His people joy, deliverance from bondage to sin, and victory over their enemies. In Deuteronomy 33, Moses blessed each of the twelve tribes of Israel and concluded with a testimony to God's righteousness. Through Jesus Christ, Christians have received joy, freedom from sin, and protection from the Evil One. And God has promised to glorify Christians when He raises us from the dead at the rapture. So those who live in right relationship with God are truly the most blessed people in the world.

Deuteronomy 34

Since that time no prophet has risen in Israel like Moses, whom the
L<small>ORD</small> knew face to face.   *—Deuteronomy 34:10*

Moses knew God "face to face," like a man knows his best friend. God revealed His name to Moses at the burning bush. He used Moses to perform amazing signs before Pharaoh and deliver Israel from Egypt. God spoke with Moses on the mountain and gave him the Law. He revealed His glory as Moses hid in the cleft of the rock. God even buried Moses after his death. God promised His people that someday a prophet like Moses would come who would speak God's words (Deuteronomy 18:18). That Prophet has come and He enables people to relate to God face-to-face. Jesus Christ paid the penalty for sin and bridged the gap between fallen humans and a perfect God. And Deuteronomy 34 isn't the last time we see Moses. He appeared on the Mount of Transfiguration to testify to Jesus Christ — the Messiah, the final Prophet like Moses.

How to Begin a Relationship with God

The Bible is unique among the books of the world. Oh, it contains similar literature as other books—story, biography, history, poetry, romance, advice, apocalypse—but it's a book to be read for more than enjoyment or interest. It's a book intended to change lives. The purpose of the Bible isn't the transfer of mere knowledge about God and His activities in human history. Rather, the purpose of the Bible is the transformation of dead souls into living souls. It's a manual for how to live a life that matters eternally. But like any good manual, simply reading it is insufficient; it must be applied in the real world. And the first and greatest application anyone should make is the application of salvation. From Genesis to Revelation, God reveals four essential truths we all must accept and apply if we are to find the life-transforming remedy for our dead souls. Let's look at these four truths in detail.

Our Spiritual Condition: Totally Depraved

The first truth is rather personal. One look in the mirror of Scripture, and our human condition becomes painfully clear:

> "There is none righteous, not even one;
> There is none who understands,
> There is none who seeks for God;
> All have turned aside, together they have
>   become useless;
> There is none who does good,
> There is not even one." (Romans 3:10–12)

We are all sinners through and through—totally depraved. Now, that doesn't mean we've committed every atrocity known to humankind. We're not as *bad* as we can be, just as *bad off* as we can be. Sin colors all our thoughts, motives, words, and actions.

If you've been around a while, you likely already believe it. Look around. Everything around us bears the smudge marks of our sinful nature. Despite our best efforts to create a perfect world, crime statistics continue to soar, divorce rates keep climbing, and families keep crumbling.

Something has gone terribly wrong in our society and in ourselves—something deadly. Contrary to how the world would repackage it, "me-first" living doesn't equal rugged individuality and freedom; it equals death. As Paul said in his letter to the Romans, "The wages of sin is death" (Romans 6:23)—our spiritual and physical death that comes from God's righteous judgment of our sin, along with all of the emotional and practical effects of this separation that we experience on a daily basis. This brings us to the second marker: God's character.

God's Character: Infinitely Holy

How can God judge us for a sinful state we were born into? Our total depravity is only half the answer. The other half is God's infinite holiness.

The fact that we know things are not as they should be points us to a standard of goodness beyond ourselves. Our sense of injustice in life on this side of eternity implies a perfect standard of justice beyond our reality. That standard and source is God Himself. And God's standard of holiness contrasts starkly with our sinful condition.

Scripture says that "God is Light, and in Him there is no darkness at all" (1 John 1:5). God is absolutely holy—which creates a problem for us. If He is so pure, how can we who are so impure relate to Him?

Perhaps we could try being better people, try to tilt the balance in favor of our good deeds, or seek out methods for self-improvement. Throughout history, people have attempted to live up to God's standard by keeping the Ten Commandments or living by their own code of ethics. Unfortunately, no one can come close to satisfying the demands of God's law. Romans 3:20 says, "By the works of the Law no flesh will be justified in His sight; for through the Law comes the knowledge of sin."

Our Need: A Substitute

So here we are, sinners by nature and sinners by choice, trying to pull ourselves up by our own bootstraps to attain a relationship with our holy Creator. But every time we try, we fall flat on our faces. We can't live a good enough life to make up for our sin, because God's standard isn't "good enough"—it's *perfection*. And we can't make amends for the offense our sin has created without dying for it.

Who can get us out of this mess?

If someone could live perfectly, honoring God's law, and would bear sin's death penalty for us—in our place—then we would be saved from our predicament. But is there such a person? Thankfully, yes!

Meet your substitute—*Jesus Christ*. He is the One who took death's place for you!

[God] made [Jesus Christ] who knew no
sin to be sin on our behalf, so that we might
become the righteousness of God in Him.
(2 Corinthians 5:21)

God's Provision: A Savior

God rescued us by sending His Son, Jesus, to die on the cross
for our sins (1 John 4:9–10). Jesus was fully human and fully
divine (John 1:1, 18), a truth that ensures His understanding of
our weaknesses, His power to forgive, and His ability to bridge
the gap between God and us (Romans 5:6–11). In short, we are
"justified as a gift by His grace through the redemption which
is in Christ Jesus" (Romans 3:24). Two words in this verse bear
further explanation: *justified* and *redemption*.

Justification is God's act of mercy, in which He declares righteous the believing sinners while we are still in our sinning state.
Justification doesn't mean that God *makes* us righteous, so that
we never sin again, rather that He *declares* us righteous—much
like a judge pardons a guilty criminal. Because Jesus took our
sin upon Himself and suffered our judgment on the cross, God
forgives our debt and proclaims us PARDONED.

Redemption is Christ's act of paying the complete price to
release us from sin's bondage. God sent His Son to bear His wrath
for all of our sins—past, present, and future (Romans 3:24–26;
2 Corinthians 5:21). In humble obedience, Christ willingly
endured the shame of the cross for our sake (Mark 10:45;
Romans 5:6–8; Philippians 2:8). Christ's death satisfied God's
righteous demands. He no longer holds our sins against us,
because His own Son paid the penalty for them. We are freed
from the slave market of sin, never to be enslaved again!

Placing Your Faith in Christ

These four truths describe how God has provided a way to Himself through Jesus Christ. Because the price has been paid in full by God, we must respond to His free gift of eternal life in total faith and confidence in Him to save us. We must step forward into the relationship with God that He has prepared for us — not by doing good works or by being a good person, but by coming to Him just as we are and accepting His justification and redemption by faith.

> For by grace you have been saved through faith;
> and that not of yourselves, it is the gift of God;
> not as a result of works, so that no one may
> boast. (Ephesians 2:8–9)

We accept God's gift of salvation simply by placing our faith in Christ alone for the forgiveness of our sins. Would you like to enter a relationship with your Creator by trusting in Christ as your Savior? If so, here's a simple prayer you can use to express your faith:

> *Dear God,*
>
> *I know that my sin has put a barrier between You and me. Thank You for sending Your Son, Jesus, to die in my place. I trust in Jesus alone to forgive my sins, and I accept His gift of eternal life. I ask Jesus to be my personal Savior and the Lord of my life. Thank You. In Jesus's name, amen.*

If you've prayed this prayer or one like it and you wish to find out more about knowing God and His plan for you in the Bible, contact us at Insight for Living Ministries. Our contact information is on the following pages.

We Are Here for You

If you desire to find out more about knowing God and His plan for you in the Bible, contact us. Insight for Living Ministries provides staff pastors who are available for free written correspondence or phone consultation. These seminary-trained and seasoned counselors have years of experience and are well-qualified guides for your spiritual journey.

Please feel welcome to contact your regional Pastoral Ministries by using the information below:

United States

Insight for Living
Pastoral Ministries
Post Office Box 269000
Plano, Texas 75026-9000
USA
972-473-5097, Monday through Friday,
8:00 a.m. – 5:00 p.m. central time
www.insight.org/contactapastor

Canada

Insight for Living Canada
Pastoral Ministries
PO Box 8 Stn A
Abbotsford BC V2T 6Z4
CANADA
1-800-663-7639
info@insightforliving.ca

Australia, New Zealand, and South Pacific

Insight for Living Australia
Pastoral Care
Post Office Box 443
Boronia, VIC 3155
AUSTRALIA
1300 467 444

United Kingdom and Europe

Insight for Living United Kingdom
Pastoral Care
PO Box 553
Dorking
RH4 9EU
UNITED KINGDOM
0800 787 9364
+44 (0)1306 640156
pastoralcare@insightforliving.org.uk

Endnotes

1. Adapted from Wayne Stiles, *Going Places with God: A Devotional Journey Through the Lands of the Bible* (Ventura, Calif: Regal Books, 2006), 139.

2. Earl S. Kalland, "Deuteronomy," in *The Expositor's Bible Commentary*, vol. 3, ed. Frank E. Gaebelein (Grand Rapids: Zondervan, 1988), 66.

Resources for Probing Further

Resources for how to read and study the Bible to increase your *knowledge* are readily available — you can find libraries of books that will do that. Finding resources to help you *apply* what you're learning is . . . well, a bit like exploring an empty shelf. So, to keep you from a frustrating and potentially fruitless search for resources with application as their approach, we've compiled a list of books as a place to start. Keep in mind as you read these books that we can't always endorse everything a writer or ministry says, so we encourage you to approach these and all other non-biblical resources with wisdom and discernment.

Insight for Living. *Insight's Old Testament Handbook: A Practical Look at Each Book*. Plano, Tex.: IFL Publishing House, 2009.

Insight for Living. *Joseph: A Man of Integrity and Forgiveness Bible Companion*. Plano, Tex.: IFL Publishing House, 2007.

Morgan, G. Campbell. *Life Applications from Every Chapter in the Bible*. Grand Rapids: Fleming H. Revell, 1994.

Ross, Allen P. *Creation and Blessing: A Guide to the Study and Exposition of Genesis*. Grand Rapids: Baker Academic, 1998.

Ross, Allen P. *Holiness to the Lord: A Guide to the Exposition of the Book of Leviticus*. Grand Rapids: Baker Academic, 2002.

Swindoll, Charles R. *Joseph: A Man of Integrity and Forgiveness*. Nashville: Word Publishing, 1998.

Swindoll, Charles R. *Moses: A Man of Selfless Dedication*. Nashville: Word Publishing, 1999.

Wiersbe, Warren W. *The Wiersbe Bible Commentary: Old Testament*. Colorado Springs: David C. Cook, 2007.

Wiersbe, Warren W. *With the Word: The Chapter-by-Chapter Handbook*. Nashville: Thomas Nelson, 1991.

Ordering Information

If you would like to order additional copies of *Insight's Bible Application Guide: Genesis–Deuteronomy* or order other Insight for Living Ministries resources, please contact the office that serves you.

United States

Insight for Living
Post Office Box 269000
Plano, Texas 75026-9000
USA
1-800-772-8888, Monday through Friday,
7:00 a.m.–7:00 p.m. central time
www.insight.org
www.insightworld.org

Canada

Insight for Living Canada
PO Box 8 Stn A
Abbotsford BC V2T 6Z4
CANADA
1-800-663-7639
www.insightforliving.ca

Australia, New Zealand, and South Pacific

Insight for Living Australia
Post Office Box 443
Boronia, VIC 3155
AUSTRALIA
1300 467 444
www.insight.asn.au

United Kingdom and Europe

Insight for Living United Kingdom
PO Box 553
Dorking
RH4 9EU
UNITED KINGDOM
0800 787 9364
www.insightforliving.org.uk

Other International Locations

International constituents may contact the U.S. office through
our Web site (www.insightworld.org),
mail queries, or by calling +1-972-473-5136.